WeightWatchers®
momentum™

Slow Cook It

165 All-New Slow-Cooker Recipes

About Weight Watchers

Weight Watchers International, Inc., is the world's leading provider of weight-management services, operating globally through a network of company-owned and franchise operations. Weight Watchers holds over 50,000 weekly meetings worldwide, at which members receive group support and education about healthful eating patterns, behavior modification, and physical activity. Weight-loss and weight-management results vary by individual. We recommend that you attend Weight Watchers meetings to benefit from the supportive environment you'll find there and follow the comprehensive Weight Watchers program, which includes a food plan, an activity plan, and a behavioral component. In addition, Weight Watchers offers a wide range of products, publications, and programs for people interested in weight loss and weight control. For the Weight Watchers meeting nearest you, call **1-800-651-6000.** For information about bringing Weight Watchers to your workplace, call **1-800-8AT-WORK.** Also visit us at our Web site, **WeightWatchers.com,** and look for ***Weight Watchers Magazine*** at your newsstand or in your meeting room.

OSSO BUCO-STYLE
DRUMSTICKS, PAGE 95

WEIGHT WATCHERS PUBLISHING GROUP

EDITORIAL DIRECTOR	NANCY GAGLIARDI
CREATIVE DIRECTOR	ED MELNITSKY
PHOTO EDITOR	DEBORAH HARDT
MANAGING EDITOR	SARAH WHARTON
PRODUCTION MANAGER	ALAN BIEDERMAN
EDITORIAL ASSISTANT	KRISTINA LUCARELLI
FOOD EDITOR	EILEEN RUNYAN
EDITOR	CAROL PRAGER
NUTRITION CONSULTANT	U. BEATE KRINKE
RECIPE DEVELOPERS	MAUREEN LUCHEJKO
	SALLY-JO O'BRIEN
	JEAN PELLEGRINO
	PAUL PICCUITO
	SARAH REYNOLDS
	MIRIAM RUBIN
	MARLA SOCHET
PHOTOGRAPHER	ANN STRATTON
FOOD STYLIST	MICHAEL PEDERSON
PROP STYLIST	LYNDA WHITE
DESIGNER	SHELLEY CAMHI
ART DIRECTOR	DANIELA HRITCU

ON THE COVER: From top left, clockwise:
Escarole, Bean, and Chicken Soup, page 143; Kung Pao Chicken, page 86;
Spicy "Barbecued" Brisket, page 37; Stuffed Beef Rolls, page 40

About Our Recipes

We make every effort to ensure that you will have success with our recipes. For best results and for nutritional accuracy, please keep these guidelines in mind:

• Recipes in this book have been developed for members who are following the **Momentum™** plan. We include **POINTS**® values for every recipe. **POINTS** values are assigned based on calories, fat (grams), and fiber (grams) provided for a serving size of a recipe.

• All recipes feature approximate nutritional information; our recipes are analyzed for Calories (Cal), Total Fat (Fat), Saturated Fat (Sat Fat), Trans Fat (Trans Fat), Cholesterol (Chol), Sodium (Sod), Carbohydrates (Carb), Dietary Fiber (Fib), Protein (Prot), and Calcium (Calc).

• Nutritional information for recipes that include meat, poultry, and fish are based on cooked skinless boneless portions (unless otherwise stated), with the fat trimmed.

• We recommend that you buy lean meat and poultry, then trim it of all visible fat before cooking. When poultry is cooked with the skin on, we suggest removing the skin before eating.

• Before serving, divide foods—including any vegetables, accompaniments, or sauce—into portions of equal size according to the designated number of servings per recipe.

• Any substitutions made to the ingredients will alter the "Per serving" nutritional information and may affect the **POINTS** value.

• All fresh fruits, vegetables, and greens in recipes should be rinsed before using.

• All ♥™ Filling Extra suggestions have a **POINTS** value of **0** unless otherwise stated.

• All Filling Foods are highlighted in green.

• Recipes that work with the Simply Filling techinque are indicated.

**CHICKEN AND HERB
DUMPLING STEW,
PAGE 93**

Keep Warm

Off

Contents

STUFFED BREAST OF VEAL,
PAGE 127

Introduction

Slow cookers are back in a big way. In fact, surveys show that the number of households using slow cookers has almost doubled in the past 20 years. That statistic isn't surprising when you consider the remarkable array of healthful dishes that you can make with a slow cooker and the ease of using one: Simply prepare the ingredients, pop them into the insert, select the appropriate setting, and let the cooker work its magic for the next several hours. The convenience of up-front preparation, plus the inviting aroma that permeates your home—and perhaps greets you at the end of a long day—may persuade you to never again make a stew, soup, roast, or even dessert any other way!

The principle of slow cooking is simple: The cooker generates heat, a tight-fitting lid seals in the heat, and as the food simmers, it releases steam, which over the course of several hours slowly tenderizes the food, creating rich flavors. Even better, this method of slow, high-moisture cooking allows the healthful-minded cook to produce the fabulous, rich taste of many favorite dishes without using a lot of fat. Cooked in a slow cooker, lean meats that might be tough and skinless poultry that might be bland will develop the satisfying, mouthwatering taste you'll love.

TODAY'S SLOW COOKERS

Although slow cookers have come a long way since your mother's circa 1970s version, today's appliance has basically the same parts: a metal base (which houses low-watt electric coils), a stoneware insert, and a tight-fitting glass lid. The amount of energy used is so small that a slow cooker can be safely left on while you are away from home. A bonus: The stoneware insert can double as a serving dish.

Here's what's on today's slow-cooker market:

MANUAL SLOW COOKERS feature two or three settings (high, low, warm), a dishwasher-safe stoneware insert, and a glass lid. $18–$55

PROGRAMMABLE SLOW COOKERS feature multiple time and temperature settings; a digital timer that counts down the cooking time; a control that automatically shifts the temperature to warm when the cooking time is up; a dishwasher-safe stoneware insert that's safe for microwaving, baking, and browning foods on the stovetop; and a glass lid. $40–$75

ROUND AND OVAL SLOW COOKERS are available in a number of sizes: $1^1/_2$- to $3^1/_2$-quart for 1 to 3 servings, 4- to 5-quart for 4 to 6 servings, and 5- to 7-quart for 6 or more servings.

Still have mom's slow cooker? The new slow cookers heat up more quickly than some older models. If you have a classic appliance and you're following a recipe that calls for the food to cook at the low setting, for best results set the cooker on high for the first hour of cooking; then reduce the temperature to low and complete the recipe as directed.

AS EASY AS 1, 2, 3

In addition to reading the manufacturer's instructions that come with your slow cooker, follow these steps for best results:

1 **PREP SMART** Fat retains heat better than water. This means that foods with some fat, like meat, will cook in a slow cooker faster than foods with next to no fat, like vegetables. To make sure your ingredients are evenly cooked, we suggest that you cut any vegetables—particularly root vegetables, such as carrots, potatoes, and turnips—into pieces that are a bit smaller than the meat.

2 **FILL 'ER UP** Fill the slow cooker at least one half full but no more than three quarters full (just be sure to leave 2 inches between the food and the lid). Put the ingredients that take the longest to cook—like root vegetables—on the bottom and sides of the insert for maximum exposure to the heat. Place quicker-cooking ingredients, such as fish, shellfish, and thawed frozen vegetables, toward the center.

3 **KEEP A LID ON IT** Unless the recipe instructs you to stir the food, resist the urge to lift the lid. Each time you uncover the slow cooker and stir the contents, the internal temperature drops by 10° to 15°F (thus requiring the cooking time to increase by 20 to 30 minutes). If a recipe calls for stirring or you wish to check for doneness toward the end of the cooking time, replace the lid as quickly as possible.

THE GREAT BROWNING DEBATE

Is it worth the time and effort to brown meats and veggies before slow cooking, or will your food be just as tasty if you toss everything in the pot without browning it first? The good news is that you can create delicious dishes either way. But before you choose your method, keep these points in mind:

Pro Browning meats and vegetables on the stovetop begins the process of caramelization and increases a dish's depth of flavor and color. Although some foods will brown somewhat during the slow-cooking process (particularly if they are not submerged in liquid), they will not develop the same color and flavor of foods that have been browned first on the stovetop.

Con Stovetop browning involves more prep work (and cleanup); so if you're in a rush, opt for slow-cooker recipes that don't call for browning.

SLOW-COOKER FITNESS TEST

A properly working slow cooker cooks slowly enough to allow for unattended cooking yet fast enough to keep food out of the bacteria danger zone (40° to 140°F). Here's how to determine whether your slow cooker is working properly:

- Fill it one half to two thirds full with water.
- Cover and set on low for 8 hours.
- Uncover and quickly insert an instant read-thermometer into the water. The temperature should register 185°F. If the temperature is lower, the slow cooker is not heating the food to a high enough temperature quickly enough to avoid potential food-safety problems and should be replaced.

SLOW-COOKER SAFETY Q&A

While using a slow-cooker is easy, you may have questions about slow cooking and food safety. Here are some answers:

Q: Is it safe to cook food for such long periods of time at a low temperature?
A: Yes! Slow cookers are designed to ensure that safe temperatures are reached before bacteria have time to grow. According to the USDA, bacteria in food are killed at 165°F. As long as the lid is kept on and the food is cooked for the amount of time called for, it will be safe. If you're not browning larger cuts of meat or poultry first, you might, as a precaution and to give the cooking process a head start, set the slow cooker on high for 1 to 2 hours before lowering the setting. Or prepare the recipe as directed, but bring the liquid ingredients to a simmer on the stovetop before adding them to the cooker, thereby jump-starting the heating process.

Q: Can I prep the ingredients for my slow-cooker recipe and refrigerate them in the insert overnight?
A: We don't recommend this. A chilled insert filled with uncooked ingredients will not reach the proper cooking temperature in the slow cooker in a reasonable amount of time. Instead, refrigerate the chopped ingredients in separate airtight containers overnight; then combine them in the insert when you're ready to begin cooking. You can brown vegetables ahead of time and refrigerate them overnight, but avoid browning meat and poultry ahead: Browning partially cooks food and, in the case of meat, raises the temperature to a level that might encourage bacteria to grow. Brown meat and poultry only right before you assemble the dish to be slow cooked.

Q: Can I reheat leftovers in a slow cooker?
A: Although slow cookers can keep food warm up to 2 hours, they cannot reheat refrigerated leftovers safely because they take too long to come to the appropriate temperature. So use your stovetop or microwave for reheating. (Some inserts are microwavable and ovenproof up to 400°F; check the manufacturer's instructions.)

SLOW-COOKER SMARTS

Keep these slow-cooker secrets in mind and you'll be guaranteed successful results every time.

- A stoneware insert is sensitive to dramatic changes in temperature, so to avoid breakage or cracking, do not place the hot insert directly on a very cold surface.
- Power outage? If it lasts no more than 2 hours, finish cooking the food on the stovetop. If the power is out for more than 2 hours or you are unsure how long it has been out, discard the food.
- To simplify cleanup, spray the insert with nonstick spray before adding the ingredients, or use a disposable slow-cooker nylon liner (available to fit 3- to $6^1/_2$-quart slow cookers).
- Do not put frozen ingredients in a slow cooker (they can cool the cooker and slow the cooking process). Instead, completely defrost all frozen foods—including meat, poultry, seafood, and vegetables—in the refrigerator before adding them to the slow cooker.
- When cooking larger pieces of meat or poultry, use an instant-read meat thermometer to ensure that the meat is cooked to a safe temperature. For whole poultry, insert the thermometer into a thigh, without touching the bone, and make sure the temperature has reached 180°F.
- When cooking at a high altitude, allow an additional 30 minutes for each hour of cooking time specified in the recipe.

BIG, BIG BATCHES

Have an extra-large (5- to 7-quart) slow cooker and want to double a soup or stew recipe? It's easy. Just double the ingredients, with the following exceptions:

- Increase the liquid by half (or as needed). For example, if the recipe calls for 1 cup of liquid, add only 1^1/$_2$ cups.
- With the exception of pungent spices, which should be increased only sparingly (see **SEASON LATER, NOT SOONER** below), up the seasonings and dried herbs by one quarter; then adjust to taste at the end of the cooking time.
- Up the amount of any thickening agent, such as flour, cornstarch, or cornmeal, by half, adding more at the end of the cooking time if the mixture is too thin.
- Big-batch cooking means more ingredients, which take more time to heat up, so consider getting a head start by heating the liquid ingredients on the stovetop before adding them to the slow cooker.

WANT TO MAKE A RECIPE SLOW-COOKER FRIENDLY?

If you enjoy slow cooking, the good news is that you're not limited to recipes specifically created for slow cookers. Follow these tips to adapt your favorite dishes:

PICK THE RIGHT RECIPE Slow cookers are ideal for braises, stews, and soups. Vegetarian dishes, especially those with root vegetables, also do very well in slow cookers.

SIZE TO FIT Note the number of servings your recipe makes—you may need to scale it up or down depending on the size of your slow cooker. (Oval-shaped cookers offer more cooking surface and are ideal for larger cuts of meat, whereas smaller round models are best for soups.)

REDUCE LIQUIDS Slow cooking retains more moisture than other cooking methods. That means you may want to reduce the amount of liquid in a recipe (start with half to three quarters of the amount called for). Any liquid left over after the dish has been slow cooked can be used to make a sauce. Just strain the liquid into a saucepan and simmer on the stovetop until reduced.

SEASON LATER, NOT SOONER Slow cooking mellows the seasoning of a dish, so plan to adjust the salt and pepper to taste before serving. At the beginning of the cooking time, add half the amount of dried herbs and spices called for; then taste and adjust the seasoning toward the end of the cooking time. On the other hand, flavorful spice blends, such as chili powder and curry powder, intensify with slow cooking, so use them conservatively. Fresh herbs are best added at the end of the cooking time.

ADJUST TIME AND TEMPERATURE Differences in slow-cooker models can make for variation in cooking times and temperatures. But as a general rule, cook food until tender. A recipe that calls for food to cook 1^1/$_2$ to 2 hours on the stovetop will likely take about 4 hours on high in a slow cooker. Also keep in mind that 2 hours on low translates to about 1 hour on high. To ensure that meat and poultry are properly cooked, use an instant-read thermometer to check for doneness.

SLOW-COOKER BAKING TRICKS

Yes, you can make terrific "baked" goods in a slow cooker! In fact puddings, compotes, baked custards, and flans do particularly well. Just follow these helpful hints:

- Use a 3- to 5-quart slow cooker and fill the insert one half to three quarters full.
- Avoid overbeating the batter. If using an electric mixer, follow all recommended mixing times.
- Many dessert recipes, such as custards and puddings, require cooking in a baking dish that is placed inside the stoneware insert. For more even cooking, some recipes call for enough hot or boiling water to be added to the insert until it reaches halfway up the outside of the baking dish. Add water to the insert only if it is called for in the recipe.
- Don't be tempted to double a dessert recipe: it's best to simply prepare the original recipe as many times as needed to serve more people.

FROM TOP:
BROCCOLI FRITTATA
BITES, PAGE 23,
PORK-PINEAPPLE
SKEWERS, PAGE 19,
AND MOO SHU ROLLS,
PAGE 18

Chapter 1

Snacks and Drinks

Your cooker may be slow,
but it's sure to get any gathering going
with a tasty selection of easy nibbles
and specialty drinks.

Moo Shu Rolls

- ◆ 1/2 pound ground lean beef (7% fat or less)
- ◆ 1/2 pound ground lean pork
- ◆ 1 large portobello mushroom cap, finely chopped
- ◆ 1 small onion, finely chopped
- 5 garlic cloves, finely chopped
- ◆ 1/4 cup low-sodium chicken broth
- 2 tablespoons low-sodium soy sauce
- 2 tablespoons rice vinegar
- 1/2 teaspoon ground ginger
- 1/4 teaspoon five-spice powder
- ◆ 20 Boston or Bibb lettuce leaves
- ◆ 3 carrots, shredded
- ◆ 10 thin scallions, sliced
- ◆ 5 radishes, thinly sliced

1 Combine beef, pork, mushroom, onion, and garlic in 5- or 6-quart slow cooker. Mix broth, soy sauce, vinegar, ginger, and five-spice powder in small bowl; pour over beef mixture. Cover and cook until flavors are blended and sauce is slightly thickened, 4–5 hours on high or 8–10 hours on low.

2 Spoon 1 generous tablespoon beef mixture in center of each lettuce leaf. Top each with about 1 tablespoon carrots, 1 tablespoon scallion, and 1 tablespoon radishes; roll up.

This recipe works with the Simply Filling technique.

PER SERVING (2 rolls): 94 Cal, 3 g Fat, 1 g Sat Fat, 0 g Trans Fat, 27 mg Chol, 144 mg Sod, 5 g Carb, 1 g Fib, 11 g Prot, 32 mg Calc. *POINTS value: 2.*

Pork-Pineapple Skewers

prep 20 min • **cook/slow-cook** 4 hrs 5 min • **serves** 8

- ♦ 1   pound boneless pork loin, trimmed and cut into ³⁄₄-inch cubes
- 2   tablespoons cornstarch
- 2   teaspoons Asian (dark) sesame oil
- 2   (8-ounce) cans pineapple chunks in juice
- ♦ 1   red onion, chopped
- ♦ 1   yellow bell pepper, diced
- ¼   cup ketchup
- 3   tablespoons rice vinegar
- 3   tablespoons honey
- 2   tablespoons low-sodium soy sauce
- 3   garlic cloves, minced
- 1   tablespoon minced peeled fresh ginger
- 2   tablespoons chopped fresh cilantro

1 Mix pork and 1 tablespoon cornstarch in large bowl. Heat oil in large nonstick skillet over medium-high heat. Add pork and cook, turning frequently, until browned, 3–4 minutes.

2 Drain pineapple, reserving juice from 1 can. (Refrigerate juice from remaining can for another use.) Combine remaining 1 tablespoon cornstarch, pineapple and reserved juice, onion, bell pepper, ketchup, vinegar, honey, soy sauce, garlic, and ginger in 5- or 6-quart slow cooker. Stir in pork. Cover and cook until pork is fork-tender, 4–5 hours on high or 8–10 hours on low.

3 At end of cooking time, stir cilantro into slow cooker. Thread pork and pineapple evenly on 8 (12-inch) wooden skewers. Serve with sauce.

PER SERVING (1 skewer with about 2 tablespoons sauce): 159 Cal, 3 g Fat, 1 g Sat Fat, 0 g Trans Fat, 32 mg Chol, 379 mg Sod, 21 g Carb, 1 g Fib, 12 g Prot, 12 mg Calc. *POINTS value: 3.*

Chicken, Apple, and Cheese Meatballs

prep 20 min • slow-cook 4 hrs • serves 12

- ◆ 1   pound ground skinless chicken breast
- ◆ 1   small onion, finely chopped
- ◆ 1   green apple, peeled and shredded
- ½   cup whole wheat bread crumbs (1 slice)
- ½   cup shredded low-fat Cheddar cheese
- ¼   cup finely chopped fresh parsley
- 2   tablespoons grated Parmesan cheese
- ◆ 1   large egg
- ¾   teaspoon salt
- ¾   teaspoon dried thyme

1 Combine all ingredients in large bowl. Form into 36 meatballs.

2 Transfer meatballs to 5- or 6-quart slow cooker. Cover and cook until instant-read thermometer inserted in center of meatball registers 170°F, 4–5 hours on high or 8–10 hours on low. Serve with toothpicks.

IN THE KITCHEN

Before rolling the meatballs, wet your hands with water so the chicken mixture will be less sticky.

PER SERVING (3 meatballs): 82 Cal, 2 g Fat, 1 g Sat Fat, 0 g Trans Fat, 43 mg Chol, 250 mg Sod, 4 g Carb, 1 g Fib, 11 g Prot, 61 mg Calc.
POINTS value: 2.

Zesty Sausage and Tomato

prep 15 min • **cook/slow-cook** 2 hr 5 min • **serves** 12

1   pound hot Italian turkey sausage links, casings removed

♦ 1   small red onion, finely chopped

♦ 1   carrot, finely chopped

♦ 1   red bell pepper, finely chopped

♦ 1   (28-ounce) can crushed tomatoes with roasted garlic

♦ 1   (6-ounce) can tomato paste with Italian seasonings

1   teaspoon dried oregano

1   teaspoon fennel seeds

1   teaspoon sugar

¼   teaspoon black pepper

24   baked whole wheat pita chips

1 Heat large nonstick skillet over medium-high heat. Add sausage, onion, carrot, and bell pepper; cook, breaking sausage apart with wooden spoon, until sausage is well browned, 7–8 minutes.

2 Transfer sausage mixture to 5- or 6-quart slow cooker. Stir in crushed tomatoes, tomato paste, oregano, fennel seeds, sugar, and black pepper. Cover and cook until mixture simmers and thickens, 2–3 hours on high or 4–6 hours on low. Serve with pita chips.

♦ FILLING EXTRA

Prefer a mellower taste? At the end of the cooking time, stir 1 (8-ounce) package shredded fat-free mozzarella cheese into the slow cooker until the cheese melts. (The per-serving **POINTS** value will increase by **1**).

PER SERVING (⅓ cup with 2 pita chips): 149 Cal, 8 g Fat, 3 g Sat Fat, 0 g Trans Fat, 16 mg Chol, 593 mg Sod, 12 g Carb, 2 g Fib, 7 g Prot, 40 mg Calc. **POINTS** value: 3.

Baja Shrimp Boil

◆ 1   pound unpeeled large shrimp

3/4   cup dry white wine

4   tablespoons chopped fresh
    flat-leaf parsley

4   tablespoons snipped fresh dill

Grated zest of 1 lemon

1 1/2 teaspoons butter

1/2   teaspoon salt

1/4   teaspoon black pepper

1 Combine shrimp, wine, 2 tablespoons parsley, 2 tablespoons dill, lemon zest, butter, salt, and pepper in 5- or 6-quart slow cooker. Cover and cook until shrimp are just opaque in center and can be peeled easily, 2–3 hours on high or 4–6 hours on low.

2 At end of cooking time, stir remaining 2 tablespoons parsley and 2 tablespoons dill into slow cooker. Divide shrimp and cooking liquid evenly among 4 bowls.

◆ **FILLING EXTRA**

For a heartier snack, serve this saucy shrimp with 4 hot cooked small red potatoes (1 cooked potato per serving will increase the *POINTS* value by *1)*.

PER SERVING (about 6 shrimp with 3 tablespoons cooking liquid): 80 Cal, 2 g Fat, 1 g Sat Fat, 0 g Trans Fat, 110 mg Chol, 432 mg Sod, 2 g Carb, 0 g Fib, 12 g Prot, 33 mg Calc. *POINTS* value: *2.*

Broccoli Frittata Bites

prep 15 min • cook/slow-cook 3 hrs 20 min • serves 10

2   teaspoons olive oil

♦ 1   large onion, chopped

♦ 1   (10-ounce) box frozen chopped broccoli, thawed and drained

1¼ cups low-fat buttermilk

♦ 3   large eggs

½   cup all-purpose flour

1   teaspoon baking soda

½   teaspoon salt

¼   teaspoon freshly grated nutmeg

1   cup shredded low-fat Cheddar cheese

1 Spray 5- or 6-quart slow cooker stoneware with nonstick spray.

2 Heat oil in large nonstick skillet over medium heat. Add onion and cook, stirring occasionally, until softened, about 3 minutes. Reduce heat and cook, stirring occasionally, until golden and very soft, about 15 minutes. Add broccoli and cook, stirring occasionally, until flavors are blended, 2–3 minutes.

3 Whisk buttermilk and eggs in medium bowl. Whisk in flour, baking soda, salt, and nutmeg just until blended. Stir in broccoli mixture and ¾ cup Cheddar until combined.

4 Transfer mixture to slow cooker; sprinkle remaining ¼ cup Cheddar over top. Cover and cook until toothpick inserted into center comes out clean, 3–4 hours on high or 6–8 hours on low.

5 Transfer stoneware to rack and let frittata cool slightly, about 15 minutes. Cut frittata into 10 pieces. Serve warm or at room temperature.

♦ FILLING EXTRA
Prepare the recipe as directed but add 1 cup shredded carrots with the broccoli in step 2.

PER SERVING (1 piece): 100 Cal, 4 g Fat, 1 g Sat Fat, 0 g Trans Fat, 67 mg Chol, 406 mg Sod, 9 g Carb, 1 g Fib, 7 g Prot, 136 mg Calc.
POINTS value: 2.

Mini Falafels

prep 20 min · cook/slow-cook 2 hrs 10 min · serves 10

- ♦ 1 (15-ounce) can chickpeas, rinsed and drained
- ♦ 1 small onion, coarsely chopped
- ½ cup whole wheat bread crumbs (1 slice)
- ¼ cup fresh cilantro or parsley leaves
- ♦ 1 large egg
- Juice of 1 lemon
- 2 garlic cloves
- 1½ teaspoons garam masala
- ¾ teaspoon salt
- ¼ teaspoon black pepper
- 2 teaspoons olive oil

1 Put chickpeas, onion, bread crumbs, cilantro, egg, lemon juice, garlic, garam masala, salt, and pepper in food processor and pulse until coarsely chopped. With moistened hands, form into 20 patties.

2 Heat 1 teaspoon oil in large nonstick skillet over medium-high heat. Add 10 patties and cook until browned, about 3 minutes per side. Transfer patties to 5- or 6-quart slow cooker. Repeat with remaining 1 teaspoon oil and 10 patties.

3 Cover and cook until falafels are firm and heated through, 2–3 hours on high or 4–6 hours on low.

♦ **FILLING EXTRA**
Top each falafel with **1 tablespoon** plain fat-free yogurt **and a sprinkling of finely chopped fresh cilantro.**

PER SERVING (2 falafels): 76 Cal, 2 g Fat, 0 g Sat Fat, 0 g Trans Fat, 21 mg Chol, 239 mg Sod, 11 g Carb, 2 g Fib, 4 g Prot, 25 mg Calc. *POINTS* value: *1.*

Caponata

1 tablespoon olive oil

♦ **1** eggplant, diced

♦ **1** onion, chopped

1/2 teaspoon salt

♦ **1** (14 1/2-ounce) can diced tomatoes

♦ **1** large red bell pepper, chopped

♦ **3** celery stalks, thinly sliced

2 tablespoons red-wine vinegar

♦ **2** tablespoons tomato paste

3 garlic cloves, finely chopped

1/2 teaspoon dried thyme

1/2 cup chopped fresh basil

♦ **1/4** cup brine-cured Kalamata olives, pitted and chopped

1 Heat oil in large nonstick skillet over medium-high heat. Add eggplant, onion, and salt; cook, stirring occasionally, until vegetables are softened, about 6 minutes.

2 Transfer eggplant mixture to 5- or 6-quart slow cooker. Stir in tomatoes, bell pepper, celery, vinegar, tomato paste, garlic, and thyme. Cover and cook until vegetables are fork-tender, 3–4 hours on high or 6–8 hours on low.

3 Transfer caponata to large bowl and let cool to room temperature. Stir in basil and olives.

♦ **FILLING EXTRA**
Serve caponata atop 4 cups cooked whole wheat couscous (1/2 cup cooked couscous per serving will up the *POINTS* value by *2*). This recipe works with the Simply Filling technique.

PER SERVING (3/4 cup): 74 Cal, 3 g Fat, 0 g Sat Fat, 0 g Trans Fat, 0 mg Chol, 308 mg Sod, 12 g Carb, 4 g Fib, 2 g Prot, 44 mg Calc. *POINTS* value: *1*.

Black Bean Salsa Dip

prep 10 min • slow-cook 1 hr • serves 6

- ◆ 2 (15½-ounce) cans low-sodium black beans, rinsed and drained
- ◆ 1 cup fat-free salsa
-   1 teaspoon ground cumin
-   1 garlic clove, finely chopped
-   Grated zest and juice of 1 lime
-   ¼ cup chopped fresh cilantro
- ◆ ¼ cup sliced scallions
- ◆ 24 celery sticks

1 Combine beans, salsa, cumin, and garlic in 5- or 6-quart slow cooker. Cover and cook until beans are hot, 1–2 hours on high or 2–4 hours on low.

2 At end of cooking time, stir lime juice and zest into slow cooker. With large spoon or potato masher, coarsely mash bean mixture. Stir in cilantro and scallions. Serve warm with celery sticks.

◆ **FILLING EXTRA**

For a cheesy-topped dip, prepare the recipe as directed, but after stirring in the cilantro and scallions, sprinkle the bean mixture with ½ cup shredded fat-free mozzarella cheese. Cover and cook on high until the cheese melts, about 10 minutes. This recipe works with the Simply Filling technique.

PER SERVING (½ cup salsa with 4 celery sticks): 159 Cal, 1 g Fat, 0 g Sat Fat, 0 g Trans Fat, 0 mg Chol, 275 mg Sod, 30 g Carb, 12 g Fib, 9 g Prot, 96 mg Calc. *POINTS* value: 2.

Tomatillo-Pinto Bean Dip

prep 10 min • **slow-cook** 1 hr • **serves** 6

- ◆ 2 (15-ounce) cans pinto beans, rinsed and drained
- ◆ 1 (12-ounce) can tomatillos, drained and chopped
- ◆ 1 (4½-ounce) can chopped green chiles
- ◆ 1 small red onion, chopped
- ◆ ¼ cup vegetable broth or water
- 1 tablespoon cider vinegar
- 1 teaspoon chili powder
- ½ teaspoon ground cumin
- ½ teaspoon salt
- ⅛ teaspoon cayenne
- ¼ cup chopped fresh cilantro
- Juice of 1 lime
- ◆ 24 jicama sticks

1 Combine beans, tomatillos, chiles, onion, broth, vinegar, chili powder, cumin, salt, and cayenne in 5- or 6-quart slow cooker. Cover and cook until slightly thickened, 1–2 hours on high or 2–4 hours on low.

2 At end of cooking time, stir cilantro and lime juice into slow cooker. Let mixture cool about 5 minutes. Puree in batches in food processor. Serve warm or at room temperature with jicama sticks.

IN THE KITCHEN

If you want to make this dip ahead, transfer to an airtight container and let cool completely. Cover and refrigerate up to 4 days. Let return to room temperature before serving. This recipe works with the Simply Filling technique.

PER SERVING (⅓ cup with 4 jicama sticks): 173 Cal, 1 g Fat, 0 g Sat Fat, 0 g Trans Fat, 0 mg Chol, 519 g Sod, 33 g Carb, 11 g Fib, 10 g Prot, 63 mg Calc. *POINTS* value: *3.*

Warm Cheese and Cannellini Dip

prep 10 min • **slow-cook** 1 hr • **serves** 12

♦ 3 (15½-ounce) cans cannellini (white kidney) beans, rinsed and drained

½ cup water

½ cup grated pecorino cheese

3 garlic cloves, thinly sliced

2 tablespoons olive oil

2 teaspoons Italian seasoning

¼ teaspoon salt

¼ teaspoon black pepper

Grated zest and juice of 1 small lemon

♦ 24 slices fennel

1 Combine beans, water, pecorino, garlic, oil, Italian seasoning, salt, and pepper in 5- or 6-quart slow cooker. Cover and cook until percorino melts and garlic is softened, 1–2 hours on high or 2–4 hours on low.

2 At end of cooking time, stir lemon zest and juice into slow cooker. With large spoon or potato masher, coarsely mash bean mixture. Serve warm or at room temperature with fennel slices.

IN THE KITCHEN

To make ahead, transfer this dip to a microwavable container and let cool. Cover and refrigerate up to 3 days. To serve, microwave, partially covered, on High until heated through, about 3 minutes, stirring once halfway through the cooking time.

PER SERVING (¼ cup with 2 fennel slices): 148 Cal, 4 g Fat, 1 g Sat Fat, 0 g Trans Fat, 5 mg Chol, 296 mg Sod, 21 g Carb, 6 g Fib, 9 g Prot, 101 mg Calc. *POINTS value: 2.*

Southern Artichoke Dip

- ♦ 2 (14-ounce) cans artichoke hearts, drained and finely chopped
- ♦ 1 (10-ounce) package frozen chopped collard greens, thawed and squeezed dry
- 1 cup grated Parmesan cheese
- 1 cup low-fat mayonnaise
- 1/2 cup light sour cream
- 2 shallots, chopped
- 1/4 teaspoon hot pepper sauce

Grated zest of 1/2 lemon

- ♦ 2 red bell peppers, cut into strips

1 Combine artichoke hearts, collard greens, Parmesan, mayonnaise, sour cream, shallots, and pepper sauce in 5- or 6-quart slow cooker. Cover and cook until Parmesan melts and dip is hot, 1–2 hours on high or 3–4 hours on low.

2 At end of cooking time, stir lemon zest into slow cooker. Serve with bell pepper strips.

IN THE KITCHEN

If you like, substitute a package of frozen chopped spinach or Swiss chard, thawed and squeezed dry, for the collard greens.

PER SERVING (1/3 cup with about 3 bell pepper strips): 128 Cal, 7 g Fat, 3 g Sat Fat, 0 g Trans Fat, 10 mg Chol, 464 mg Sod, 13 g Carb, 5 g Fib, 6 g Prot, 180 mg Calc. *POINTS* value: *2.*

Italian Snack Mix

prep 5 min • slow-cook 2 hrs 50 min • serves 20

1/4 cup light stick butter

1/4 cup grated Parmesan cheese

1 teaspoon garlic powder

1 teaspoon Italian seasoning

8 cups multigrain oat cereal

2 cups tiny pretzel twists

2 cups goldfish cheese crackers

12 dried apricots, chopped

1 Place butter in 5- or 6-quart slow cooker. Cover and cook until melted, about 5 minutes on high. Add Parmesan, garlic powder, and Italian seasoning; mix well. Stir in cereal, pretzels, cheese crackers, and apricots.

2 Cook uncovered on high about 45 minutes, stirring every 15 minutes.

3 Reduce heat to low. Cook uncovered, stirring occasionally, until mixture is crisp and fragrant, 2–3 hours. Transfer mixture to large bowl and let cool completely.

PER SERVING (1/2 cup): 115 Cal, 3 g Fat, 1 g Sat Fat, 0 g Trans Fat, 5 mg Chol, 226 mg Sod, 20 g Carb, 2 g Fib, 3 g Prot, 70 mg Calc. *POINTS* value: *2.*

Hot Chocolate Latte

¾ cup confectioners' sugar

¼ cup unsweetened cocoa

½ teaspoon cinnamon

¼ teaspoon salt

2 cups low-fat (1%) milk

6 cups brewed coffee

2 tablespoons semisweet chocolate chips

1 teaspoon vanilla extract

Whisk sugar, cocoa, cinnamon, and salt in 5- or 6-quart slow cooker until smooth. Whisk in milk until blended. Stir in coffee, chocolate chips, and vanilla. Cover and cook until hot and flavors are blended, 1–2 hours on high or 2–4 hours on low. Ladle into mugs.

IN THE KITCHEN

Having a party? You can keep the latte hot in the slow cooker on low or warm up to 3 hours.

PER SERVING (generous 1 cup): 123 Cal, 2 g Fat, 1 g Sat Fat, 0 g Trans Fat, 4 mg Chol, 140 mg Sod, 25 g Carb, 3 g Fib, 4 g Prot, 109 mg Calc.
POINTS value: 2.

Mumbai Chai

prep 10 min • slow-cook 1 hr • serves 8

6   cups low-fat (1%) milk

2   cups water

½   cup packed brown sugar

6   Darjeeling tea bags

8   whole cloves

8   cardamom pods

2   whole cinnamon sticks

1   (2-inch) piece peeled fresh ginger, sliced

2   teaspoons vanilla extract

1 Whisk milk, water, and brown sugar in 5- or 6-quart slow cooker until smooth. Stir in tea bags, cloves, cardamom, cinnamon sticks, ginger, and vanilla. Cover and cook until hot and flavors are blended, 1–2 hours on high or 2–4 hours on low.

2 Pour chai through strainer into large heatproof bowl. Discard tea bags, cloves, cardamom, cinnamon sticks, and ginger. Ladle into mugs.

IN THE KITCHEN

To make serving easier, prepare the recipe as directed, but wrap the tea bags, cloves, cardamom, cinnamon sticks, and ginger in a cheesecloth bag tied with kitchen string. Then all you need to do is remove the bag with a slotted spoon in step 2 and serve the chai from the slow cooker.

PER SERVING (1 cup): 135 Cal, 2 g Fat, 1 g Sat Fat, 0 g Trans Fat, 9 mg Chol, 90 mg Sod, 23 g Carb, 0 g Fib, 6 g Prot, 231 mg Calc. *POINTS* value: *3.*

Glogg

4 cups red wine

1 cup vodka

Zest of 1 orange, removed in strips with vegetable peeler

Zest of 2 lemons, removed in strips with vegetable peeler

4 (3-inch) cinnamon sticks

2 tablespoons sugar

12 cardamom pods

1 tablespoon whole cloves

1/4 cup slivered almonds

2 tablespoons raisins

1 Combine wine, vodka, orange and lemon zests, cinnamon sticks, sugar, cardamom, and cloves in 4- or 5-quart slow cooker. Cover and cook until hot and flavors are blended, 2–3 hours on high or 4–6 hours on low.

2 Remove orange and lemon zest strips, cinnamon stick, cardamom, and cloves with slotted spoon and discard. Divide almonds and raisins among 8 heat-resistant glasses or mugs then top evenly with glogg.

PER SERVING (about 1/2 cup): 194 Cal, 2 g Fat, 0 g Sat Fat, 0 g Trans Fat, 0 mg Chol, 6 mg Sod, 6 g Carb, 1 g Fib, 1 g Prot, 21 mg Calc.
POINTS value: 4.

SOUTHWEST STEAK TACOS,
PAGE 39

Chapter 2

Beef, Pork and More

Love meat? Assemble your ingredients and let the satisfying aromas from your favorite dinners greet you at the door.

Harvest Pot Roast Dinner

prep 25 min • **cook/slow-cook** 5 hrs 15 min • **serves** 6

- 1 (1¼-pound) bottom round steak, trimmed
- ½ **teaspoon salt**
- ½ **teaspoon black pepper**
- 2 **teaspoons olive oil**
- 2 large onions, sliced
- 3 **garlic cloves, thinly sliced**
- 2 cups low-sodium beef broth
- 3 tablespoons tomato paste
- 3 large carrots, cut diagonally into ½-inch slices
- 2 stalks celery, cut diagonally into ½-inch slices
- 8 **thyme sprigs, tied with kitchen string**
- 1 **bay leaf**
- 1 pound baby red potatoes, scrubbed and halved

1 Sprinkle beef with salt and pepper. Heat oil in large nonstick skillet over medium-high heat. Add beef and cook until browned, 3–4 minutes per side. Transfer beef to 5- or 6-quart slow cooker.

2 Spray skillet with nonstick spray and set over medium heat. Add onions and garlic; cover and cook, stirring occasionally, until onions are softened and lightly browned, about 8 minutes. Transfer onion mixture to slow cooker.

3 Combine 1 cup broth and tomato paste in skillet. Bring to boil, whisking constantly, about 1 minute. Pour broth mixture into slow cooker. Stir in remaining 1 cup broth, carrots, celery, thyme, and bay leaf. Press potatoes down into vegetable mixture. Cover and cook until beef and vegetables are fork-tender, 5–6 hours on high or 10–12 hours on low.

4 Transfer beef to cutting board and let stand 10 minutes. Transfer vegetables with slotted spoon to bowl. Discard thyme and bay leaf. Cut beef across grain into 12 slices. Serve with vegetables and gravy.

This recipe works with the Simply Filling technique.

PER SERVING (2 slices beef with generous ¾ cup vegetables and scant 3 tablespoons gravy): 279 Cal, 6 g Fat, 2 g Sat Fat, 0 g Trans Fat, 68 mg Chol, 362 mg Sod, 25 g Carb, 4 g Fib, 31 g Prot, 57 mg Calc. *POINTS* value: 5.

Country Captain Chicken

prep 25 min • **slow-cook** 3 hrs • **serves** 8

- 1 (14$\frac{1}{2}$-ounce) can fire-roasted diced tomatoes with garlic
- 1 onion, quartered and thinly sliced
- 1 yellow or red bell pepper, coarsely chopped
- 2 tablespoons tomato paste
- 1 tablespoon grated peeled fresh ginger
- 2 teaspoons curry powder
- $\frac{1}{2}$ teaspoon cinnamon
- $\frac{1}{2}$ teaspoon salt
- 1 (3$\frac{1}{2}$-pound) chicken, cut into 8 pieces and skinned
- 2 tablespoons cold water
- 1 tablespoon cornstarch
- 1 Granny Smith apple, peeled and thinly sliced
- 1 cup frozen edamame or peas, thawed
- 4 teaspoons toasted coconut
- 4 teaspoons dried currants

1 Combine tomatoes, onion, bell pepper, tomato paste, ginger, curry powder, cinnamon, and salt in 5- or 6-quart slow cooker. Top with chicken. Cover and cook until chicken is fork-tender, 3–4 hours on high or 6–8 hours on low.

2 About 25 minutes before cooking time is up, mix water and cornstarch in small bowl until smooth. Stir cornstarch mixture, apple, and edamame into slow cooker. Cover and cook on high until mixture simmers and thickens and apples are just tender, about 20 minutes. Serve, sprinkled with coconut and currants.

♦ FILLING EXTRA
Country Captain is traditionally served with white rice, but our healthful version is equally tasty accompanied by 4 cups cooked brown rice ($\frac{1}{2}$ cup cooked rice for each serving will increase the **POINTS** value by **2**).

PER SERVING (1 piece chicken with about $\frac{2}{3}$ cup vegetables and sauce and $\frac{1}{2}$ teaspoon each coconut and currants): 224 Cal, 8 g Fat, 2 g Sat Fat, 0 g Trans Fat, 71 mg Chol, 325 mg Sod, 13 g Carb, 3 g Fib, 26 g Prot, 54 mg Calc. **POINTS** value: **5.**

Chicken with Fennel and Orange

- ♦ 1   cup low-sodium chicken broth
-    8   small shallots, peeled
- ♦ 3   carrots, sliced
-    3/4   teaspoon crushed dried rosemary
-    3/4   teaspoon salt
-    1/4   teaspoon black pepper
- ♦ 1   (3- to 3 1/2-pound) chicken, wings discarded, cut into 6 pieces, and skinned
- ♦ 1   (1-pound) fennel bulb, halved and cut into 16 wedges through the root end
- ♦ 1   navel orange

1 Combine broth, shallots, carrots, rosemary, salt, and pepper in 5- or 6-quart slow cooker. Top with chicken and fennel. Cover and cook until chicken and vegetables are fork-tender, 3–4 hours on high or 6–8 hours on low.

2 Meanwhile, grate zest from half of orange; transfer to small bowl. Remove peel and pith from orange. Cut orange in half; thickly slice and combine with zest.

3 Transfer chicken to cutting board; cut each breast in half the short way. Transfer chicken to platter. Stir orange mixture into slow cooker; pour over chicken.

♦ **FILLING EXTRA**

Perk up the flavor of this Mediterranean-inspired dish by adding 8 brine-cured Kalamata olives, pitted and chopped with the orange mixture in step 3. This recipe works with the Simply Filling technique.

PER SERVING (2 pieces chicken with 1 cup vegetables and sauce): 357 Cal, 11 g Fat, 3 g Sat Fat, 0 g Trans Fat, 121 mg Chol, 656 mg Sod, 22 g Carb, 5 g Fib, 43 g Prot, 109 mg Calc. *POINTS* value: 7.

Apple Cider Chicken

prep 25 min • **slow-cook** 3 hrs • **serves** 4

- 3   parsnips, peeled, halved lengthwise, and sliced
- 2   sweet potatoes, peeled and cut into 1-inch chunks
- 1   onion, quartered and thinly sliced
- 3/4   cup apple cider
- 2   tablespoons whole-grain mustard
- 2   garlic cloves, thinly sliced
- 1   teaspoon dried thyme
- 3/4   teaspoon salt
- 2   (3/4-pound) bone-in chicken breasts, skinned
- 2   tablespoons cold water
- 1   tablespoon cornstarch
- 1   Gala or Fuji apple, peeled and thinly sliced
- 1/4   cup fat-free sour cream

1 Combine parsnips, potatoes, onion, cider, mustard, garlic, thyme, and salt in 5- or 6-quart slow cooker. Top with chicken. Cover and cook until chicken and vegetables are fork-tender, 3–4 hours on high or 6–8 hours on low.

2 About 25 minutes before cooking time is up, mix water and cornstarch in small bowl until smooth. Stir cornstarch mixture and apple into slow cooker. Cover and cook on high until mixture simmers and thickens and apple is just tender, about 20 minutes.

3 Transfer chicken to cutting board; cut each breast in half the short way. Transfer chicken to platter; pour over vegetables and sauce. Serve, topped with sour cream.

◆ **FILLING EXTRA**
Add **1 peeled and thinly sliced** Bosc pear **along with the apple in step 2.**

PER SERVING (1 piece chicken with 1 cup vegetables and sauce and 1 tablespoon sour cream): 345 Cal, 5 g Fat, 1 g Sat Fat, 0 g Trans Fat, 77 mg Chol, 651 mg Sod, 45 g Carb, 7 g Fib, 31 g Prot, 102 mg Calc. *POINTS* value: 7.

Braised Chicken and Artichokes

prep 20 min • slow-cook 3 hrs • serves 4

- ♦ 1   pound baby red potatoes, scrubbed and halved
- 3/4 cup dry white wine
- 3   garlic cloves, thinly sliced
- 1 1/2 teaspoons dried tarragon
- 1   teaspoon salt
- 1/4 teaspoon black pepper
- 1/8 teaspoon ground allspice (optional)
- ♦ 2   (3/4-pound) bone-in chicken breasts, skinned
- ♦ 1   (9-ounce) box frozen artichoke hearts, thawed
- ♦ 2   cups frozen pearl onions, thawed
- 1   lemon, cut into wedges

1 Combine potatoes, wine, garlic, 1 teaspoon tarragon, salt, pepper, and allspice (if using) in 5- or 6-quart slow cooker. Top with chicken. Cover and cook until chicken and potatoes are fork-tender, 3–4 hours on high or 6–8 hours on low.

2 About 30 minutes before cooking time is up, stir artichokes and onions into slow cooker. Cover and cook on high until vegetables are tender, about 25 minutes.

3 Stir in remaining 1/2 teaspoon tarragon. Transfer chicken to cutting board; cut each breast in half the short way. Transfer chicken to platter; pour over vegetables and sauce. Serve with lemon wedges.

♦ FILLING EXTRA
Add 2 cups frozen thawed peas along with the artichokes and onions in step 2 and up the per-serving *POINTS* value by *1*.

PER SERVING (1 piece chicken with 1 3/4 cups vegetables and sauce):
376 Cal, 6 g Fat, 2 g Sat Fat, 0 g Trans Fat, 106 mg Chol, 734 mg Sod,
36 g Carb, 10 g Fib, 43 g Prot, 88 mg Calc. *POINTS* value: *7.*

157 Lentil Soup / Squash

lentils
15½ oz chick peas
fresh ginger
butternut squash
veg broth
Italian style stewed toms
1 bag 6oz baby spinach
2 10 oz froz broc, caul, carrot
   + zucchini — thawed
red pepper flakes

4

Couscous

- 1½ C water or broth
- 2 T butter
- 1 C cous,
- salt   boil
- Let stand 5 mins

Orzo

Boil 4 qts water w
2t salt   add 2t olive oil
Just before Orzo is added
stir gently   Boil 9 mins

Pumpkin cake:

1 can (29 oz) pumpkin

p 36
~~crackers~~
~~garlic~~
~~1 1/4 lb bottom round steak~~
~~onion~~
~~beef broth~~   ~~beer~~
~~carrots~~   ~~bologna~~
~~celery~~
~~sm. red potatoes~~

p 50
~~tom. paste~~
pine nuts
~~red bell pep~~
~~orzo~~
~~fat free feta~~
~~grd beef~~

157

Sears Chavari 800 927-
2291

○

thaw Broc caul
2 10 oz frog Broc caul
sweet

2 tomatu
2 sweet pot
lentils
15½ oz Chick peas
butternut squash
stewed toma
1 bag 6 oz baby spin ich

3 ~~parsnips~~
2 ~~sweet pots~~
~~onion~~
~~apple cider~~
~~chick breasts 3/4 lb - bone in~~
~~apple~~

137 Vegies
2 ~~sweet pots~~
2 ~~carrots~~
2 ~~tams~~
1 ~~parsnip~~
~~dried plums~~
~~veg. broth~~
~~couscous~~
sliced almonds

Classic Chicken Noodle Soup

prep 20 min • **slow-cook/cook** 4 hrs 25 min • **serves** 6

- ♦ 2 (1/2-pound) bone-in chicken breasts, skinned
- ♦ 1 onion, chopped
- ♦ 3 celery stalks, sliced
- ♦ 2 carrots, sliced
- 6 fresh parsley sprigs
- 2 garlic cloves, peeled
- 1 bay leaf
- 1 tablespoon chopped fresh thyme or 1 teaspoon dried
- 1/2 teaspoon salt
- 1/4 teaspoon black pepper
- ♦ 2 (32-ounce) cartons low-sodium chicken broth
- 1 1/2 cups no-yolk egg noodles
- 1/4 cup chopped fresh dill

1 Combine chicken, onion, celery, carrots, parsley, garlic, bay leaf, thyme, salt, and pepper in 5- or 6-quart slow cooker. Pour broth over chicken and vegetables. Cover and cook until chicken and vegetables are fork-tender, 4–5 hours on high or 8–10 hours on low.

2 At end of cooking time, remove parsley, garlic, and bay leaf with slotted spoon and discard. Transfer chicken to plate and let stand until cool enough to handle, about 10 minutes. Remove and discard bones from chicken; cut chicken into bite-size pieces.

3 Meanwhile, cook noodles according to package directions, omitting salt if desired.

4 Stir chicken and noodles into slow cooker. Cover and cook on high until chicken is hot, about 5 minutes. Serve, sprinkled with dill.

♦ **FILLING EXTRA**
Add 1 1/2 cups thawed frozen shelled edamame to the slow cooker with the chicken and noodles in step 4 and increase the cooking time to 15 minutes. (The per-serving **POINTS** value will increase by **1**).

PER SERVING (2 cups): 210 Cal, 4 g Fat, 2 g Sat Fat, 0 g Trans Fat, 47 mg Chol, 428 mg Sod, 21 g Carb, 2 g Fib, 23 g Prot, 72 mg Calc.
POINTS value: **4**.

Vietnamese Soupy Noodles and Chicken

prep 25 min • **slow-cook/cook** 4 hrs 30 min • **serves** 4

◆ 2 (½-pound) bone-in chicken breasts, skinned

6 fresh cilantro sprigs

◆ 3 scallions, cut and separated into white and green parts

1 lemongrass stalk, trimmed and finely chopped

2 garlic cloves, bruised

1 teaspoon coriander seeds

1 (3-inch) cinnamon stick

½ teaspoon salt

⅛ teaspoon black pepper

◆ 2 (32-ounce) cartons low-sodium chicken broth

¼ pound rice noodles

Fresh cilantro, basil, and mint sprigs, for garnish

4 lime wedges, for garnish

1 Combine chicken, 6 cilantro sprigs, white parts of scallions, lemongrass, garlic, coriander seeds, cinnamon stick, salt, and pepper in 5- or 6-quart slow cooker. Pour broth over chicken and vegetables. Cover and cook until chicken is fork-tender, 4–5 hours on high or 8–10 hours on low.

2 At end of cooking time, transfer chicken with slotted spoon to plate and let stand until cool enough to handle, about 10 minutes. Remove and discard bones from chicken; cut chicken into bite-size pieces.

3 Meanwhile, cook noodles according to package directions. Drain and rinse under cold running water. Strain broth through large sieve into large bowl. Discard vegetables and spices.

4 Stir chicken and noodles into slow cooker. Cover and cook on high until chicken and noodles are hot, about 10 minutes.

5 Finely slice green parts of scallions. Ladle soup into bowls; sprinkle evenly with scallion greens. Garnish with cilantro, basil, and mint sprigs and lime wedges.

IN THE KITCHEN
If you don't have a fine sieve to strain the broth in step 3, use a colander lined with cheesecloth.

PER SERVING (2½ cups): 293 Cal, 6 g Fat, 2 g Sat Fat, 0 g Trans Fat, 70 mg Chol, 562 mg Sod, 27 g Carb, 1 g Fib, 31 g Prot, 63 mg Calc.
POINTS value: *6.*

Chicken with Figs

♦ 1   (1¼-pound) butternut squash, peeled and cut into ¾-inch chunks

♦ 3   parsnips, peeled and sliced

½   cup dried Calimyrna figs

¼   cup + 2 tablespoons cold water

3   tablespoons packed dark brown sugar

2   tablespoons red-wine vinegar

2   garlic cloves, cut into thin strips

¾   teaspoon salt

¼   teaspoon black pepper

♦ 4   (¼-pound) skinless, boneless chicken breasts

1   tablespoon cornstarch

2   tablespoons port or unsweetened apple juice

1 Combine squash, parsnips, figs, ¼ cup water, brown sugar, vinegar, garlic, salt, and pepper in 5- or 6-quart slow cooker. Top with chicken. Cover and cook until chicken and vegetables are fork-tender, 3–4 hours on high or 6–8 hours on low.

2 About 25 minutes before cooking time is up, mix remaining 2 tablespoons water and cornstarch in small bowl until smooth. Stir cornstarch mixture and port into slow cooker. Cover and cook on high until mixture simmers and thickens, about 20 minutes.

♦ **FILLING EXTRA**
Serve this subtle fruity chicken with 2 cups cooked quinoa (½ cup for each serving will up the *POINTS* value by *2*).

PER SERVING (1 chicken breast with 1 cup vegetables and sauce): 339 Cal, 6 g Fat, 2 g Sat Fat, 0 g Trans Fat, 58 mg Chol, 508 mg Sod, 49 g Carb, 7 g Fib, 24 g Prot, 122 mg Calc. *POINTS* value: *6.*

Spanish Chicken with Chorizo

- 1 (14$\frac{1}{2}$-ounce) can diced tomatoes with basil, garlic, and oregano
- **3 tablespoons balsamic vinegar**
- 2 tablespoons tomato paste
- **1 tablespoon paprika**
- **$\frac{1}{4}$ teaspoon salt**
- 1 large onion, chopped
- 2 stalks celery, sliced
- **$\frac{1}{4}$ cup chopped chorizo sausage**
- 4 ($\frac{1}{4}$-pound) skinless, boneless chicken breasts
- 1 large yellow or red bell pepper, coarsely chopped
- 1 tablespoon cornmeal
- 1 cup frozen peas, thawed

1 Combine tomatoes, vinegar, tomato paste, paprika, and salt in 5- or 6-quart slow cooker. Stir in onion, celery, and chorizo. Top with chicken and bell pepper. Cover and cook until chicken and vegetables are fork-tender, 3–4 hours on high or 6–8 hours on low.

2 About 20 minutes before cooking time is up, gradually stir cornmeal into slow cooker until blended. Stir in peas. Cover and cook on high until mixture simmers and thickens and peas are just tender, about 15 minutes.

♦ **FILLING EXTRA**

Instead of the usual side of rice, serve this dish with 2 cups cooked instant polenta ($\frac{1}{2}$ cup cooked polenta per serving will increase the *POINTS* value by **2**).

PER SERVING (1 chicken breast with $\frac{3}{4}$ cup vegetables and sauce): 272 Cal, 6 g Fat, 2 g Sat Fat, 0 g Trans Fat, 75 mg Chol, 533 mg Sod, 22 g Carb, 5 g Fib, 31 g Prot, 83 mg Calc. *POINTS* value: *5.*

Mushroom and Cheese-Stuffed Chicken Breasts

prep 20 min • cook/slow-cook 2 hrs 10 min • serves 4

2   teaspoons olive oil

♦ 1/4   pound cremini mushrooms, finely chopped

1/2   teaspoon salt

1/4   teaspoon black pepper

2   garlic cloves, finely chopped

2   tablespoons dry vermouth

1/3   cup crumbled goat cheese with herbs

♦ 4   (1/4-pound) skinless, boneless chicken breasts

♦ 1/2   cup low-sodium chicken broth

1 To make stuffing, heat 1 teaspoon oil in medium nonstick skillet over medium-high heat. Add mushrooms, 1/4 teaspoon salt, and 1/8 teaspoon pepper; cook, stirring occasionally, until mushrooms are browned, 3–4 minutes. Add garlic and cook, stirring constantly, until fragrant, about 1 minute. Add vermouth and cook until evaporated, 1–2 minutes. Remove skillet from heat. Let mushroom mixture cool slightly, about 10 minutes. Stir in goat cheese.

2 With tip of sharp knife, cut horizontal slit through thickest portion of each chicken breast to form pocket. Fill each pocket with 2 tablespoons stuffing. Close pockets and secure with toothpicks.

3 Sprinkle chicken with remaining 1/4 teaspoon salt and 1/8 teaspoon pepper. Heat remaining 1 teaspoon oil in skillet over medium-high heat. Add chicken and cook until browned, about 2 minutes per side. Transfer chicken to 5- or 6-quart slow cooker.

4 Add broth to skillet. Bring to boil, scraping up browned bits from bottom of pan. Pour broth mixture into slow cooker. Cover and cook until chicken is fork-tender, 2–3 hours on high or 4–6 hours on low.

PER SERVING (1 chicken breast with about 2 1/2 tablespoons broth):
196 Cal, 8 g Fat, 3 g Sat Fat, 0 g Trans Fat, 71 mg Chol, 580 mg Sod,
3 g Carb, 0 g Fib, 27 g Prot, 75 mg Calc. *POINTS* value: *5.*

Kung Pao Chicken

prep 20 min • **slow-cook** 3 hrs • **serves** 4

3 tablespoons hoisin sauce

3 tablespoons dry sherry or low-sodium chicken broth

3 tablespoons ketchup

2 tablespoons low-sodium soy sauce

2 tablespoons thin strips peeled fresh ginger

1/4 teaspoon red pepper flakes

♦ 1 pound skinless, boneless chicken breasts, cut into 3/4-inch cubes

♦ 1 (8-ounce) can sliced water chestnuts, drained

2 tablespoons cold water

1 tablespoon cornstarch

♦ 3 cups frozen sliced bell peppers and onions, thawed

1 Combine hoisin sauce, sherry, ketchup, soy sauce, ginger, and red pepper flakes in 5- or 6-quart slow cooker. Stir in chicken and water chestnuts. Cover and cook until chicken is fork-tender, 3–4 hours on high or 6–8 hours on low.

2 About 20 minutes before cooking time is up, mix water and cornstarch in small bowl until smooth. Stir cornstarch mixture and bell peppers and onions into slow cooker. Cover and cook on high until mixture simmers and thickens and bell peppers and onions are crisp-tender, about 15 minutes.

IN THE KITCHEN
Like your Chinese food extra-spicy? Increase the red pepper flakes to 1/2 teaspoon.

PER SERVING (1 1/4 cups): 249 Cal, 4 g Fat, 1 g Sat Fat, 0 g Trans Fat, 71 mg Chol, 660 mg Sod, 24 g Carb, 3 g Fib, 28 g Prot, 39 mg Calc. *POINTS* value: *5.*

Jerk Chicken with Plantains

prep 20 min • **slow-cook** 3 hrs • **serves** 4

- 1   (14½-ounce) can diced tomatoes with peppers, celery, and onion
- 1   tablespoon tomato paste
- 2   garlic cloves, minced
- 2   teaspoons dry Jamaican jerk seasoning
- 2   teaspoons smoked paprika
- ½   teaspoon ground allspice
- ½   teaspoon salt
- 2   small black plantains, peeled, halved lengthwise, and sliced
- 4   (½-pound) whole chicken legs, skinned
- 2   cups frozen cut green beans, thawed

1 Combine tomatoes, tomato paste, garlic, jerk seasoning, paprika, allspice, and salt in 5- or 6-quart slow cooker. Top with plantains and chicken. Cover and cook until chicken and plantains are fork-tender, 3–4 hours on high or 6–8 hours on low.

2 About 25 minutes before cooking time is up, stir green beans into slow cooker. Cover and cook on high until green beans are crisp-tender, about 20 minutes.

PER SERVING (1 chicken leg with scant 1 cup vegetables and sauce): 349 Cal, 8 g Fat, 3 g Sat Fat, 0 g Trans Fat, 83 mg Chol, 562 mg Sod, 43 g Carb, 6 g Fib, 31 g Prot, 105 mg Calc. *POINTS* value: **7.**

African Peanut Chicken

prep 25 min · slow-cook 3 hrs · serves 8

♦ 1   (14$1/2$-ounce) can diced tomatoes with garlic and onions

♦ 4   carrots, halved lengthwise and sliced

♦ 2   parsnips, peeled, halved lengthwise, and sliced

3   tablespoons low-fat peanut butter

3   tablespoons cayenne pepper sauce

1$1/2$ teaspoons ground cumin

$1/2$ teaspoon cinnamon

♦ 4   ($1/4$-pound) skinless chicken thighs

♦ 4   ($1/4$-pound) skinless chicken drumsticks

2   tablespoons cold water

1   tablespoon cornstarch

$1/4$ cup chopped fresh cilantro (optional)

1 Combine tomatoes, carrots, parsnips, peanut butter, pepper sauce, cumin, and cinnamon in 5- or 6-quart slow cooker. Top with chicken. Cover and cook until chicken and vegetables are fork-tender, 3–4 hours on high or 6–8 hours on low.

2 About 20 minutes before cooking time is up, mix water and cornstarch in small bowl until smooth. Stir cornstarch mixture into slow cooker. Cover and cook on high until mixture simmers and thickens, about 15 minutes. Stir in cilantro (if using).

♦ FILLING EXTRA
Serve 4 cups cooked whole wheat couscous to soak up all the delicious nutty sauce ($1/2$ cup cooked couscous per serving will increase the *POINTS* value by *1*).

PER SERVING (1 piece chicken with $1/2$ cup vegetables and sauce):
172 Cal, 6 g Fat, 2 g Sat Fat, 0 g Trans Fat, 42 mg Chol, 313 mg Sod,
13 g Carb, 3 g Fib, 17 g Prot, 58 mg Calc. *POINTS* value: *3.*

Thai-Style Chicken Thighs

....
prep 20 min • **slow-cook** 3 hrs • **serves** 4
....

◆ 1   large onion, quartered and thinly sliced

  1   **cup mango or pineapple salsa**

  1   **garlic clove, finely chopped**

  3   **teaspoons Asian fish sauce**

◆ 4   (5-ounce) skinless chicken thighs

◆ 2   red bell peppers, coarsely chopped

◆ 1   green bell pepper, coarsely chopped

  ¼   **cup chopped fresh mint, basil, or cilantro**

Juice of 1 lime

1 Combine onion, salsa, garlic, and 2 teaspoons fish sauce in 5- or 6-quart slow cooker. Top with chicken and bell peppers. Cover and cook until chicken and bell peppers are fork-tender, 3–4 hours on high or 6–8 hours on low.

2 Transfer chicken to platter. Stir mint, lime juice, and remaining 1 teaspoon fish sauce into slow cooker. Pour vegetables and sauce over chicken.

◆ **FILLING EXTRA**
Serve this Thai specialty with 2 cups cooked brown basmati rice and up the per-serving *POINTS* value by *2.*

....
PER SERVING (1 chicken thigh with ¾ cup vegetables and sauce): 200 Cal, 8 g Fat, 2 g Sat Fat, 0 g Trans Fat, 57 mg Chol, 604 mg Sod, 11 g Carb, 3 g Fib, 21 g Prot, 50 mg Calc. *POINTS* value: *4.*

Tangy Cherry Chicken

- 1 cup low-sodium chicken broth
- 3 tablespoons honey
- 3 tablespoons balsamic vinegar
- $1\frac{1}{2}$ teaspoons five-spice powder or apple or pumpkin pie spice
- $3/4$ teaspoon salt
- 5 carrots, sliced
- 1 large red onion, quartered and thinly sliced
- 2 tablespoons thin strips peeled fresh ginger
- $1/2$ cup dried cherries
- 4 (5-ounce) skinless chicken thighs
- 2 tablespoons cold water
- 1 tablespoon cornstarch

1 Whisk broth, honey, $2\frac{1}{2}$ tablespoons vinegar, five-spice powder, and salt in 5- or 6-quart slow cooker. Stir in carrots, onion, and ginger. Sprinkle with cherries and top with chicken. Cover and cook until chicken and vegetables are fork-tender, 3–4 hours on high or 6–8 hours on low.

2 About 25 minutes before cooking time is up, mix water and cornstarch in small bowl until smooth. Stir cornstarch mixture into slow cooker. Cover and cook on high until mixture simmers and thickens, about 20 minutes. At end of cooking time, stir in remaining $1/2$ tablespoon vinegar.

◆ FILLING EXTRA

Round out the meal with 4 cooked small red potatoes and 4 cups steamed green beans. A cooked small potato and 1 cup cooked beans will up the *POINTS* value by *1*.

PER SERVING (1 chicken thigh with $3/4$ cup vegetables and sauce): 342 Cal, 8 g Fat, 2 g Sat Fat, 0 g Trans Fat, 57 mg Chol, 570 mg Sod, 46 g Carb, 4 g Fib, 22 g Prot, 83 mg Calc. *POINTS* value: 7.

Handwritten note card:

1. Tangy Cherry Chicken
   p 90

2 Braised chich + artichokes
   p 88

3 Country Captain Chich
   p 77

4 Ham + Veg Chowder
   p. 66

5. Pork Stew
   p 64

6 Pork Cacciatore
   p 62

Printed recipe (partially obscured):

...cken

s • **serves** 4

...ut lime into 4 wedges.

...e juice concentrate, honey, cumin, oregano, ...5- or 6-quart slow cooker. Stir in onion. Top ...sh, and zucchini. Cover and cook until chicken ...ender, 3–4 hours on high or 6–8 hours on low.

...tter. Stir cilantro into slow cooker. Pour ...er chicken. Serve with lime wedges.

¹/₄ **cup chopped fresh cilantro**

IN THE KITCHEN
Don't have chipotle chile powder on hand? Use ¹/₂ teaspoon each chili powder, smoked paprika, and your favorite brand of hot pepper sauce instead.

PER SERVING (1 chicken thigh with ³/₄ cup vegetables and sauce and 1 lime wedge): 312 Cal, 10 g Fat, 3 g Sat Fat, 0 g Trans Fat, 70 mg Chol, 518 mg Sod, 32 g Carb, 3 g Fib, 27 g Prot, 81 mg Calc. *POINTS* value: *6.*

Chicken, Sausage, and White Bean Stew

prep 30 min • **cook/slow-cook** 3 hrs 10 min • **serves** 6

♦ 4   carrots, quartered lengthwise and sliced

♦ 1   leek, cleaned and chopped, white and light green parts only

 2   garlic cloves, finely chopped

 1½ teaspoons herbes de Provence or Italian seasoning

♦ 3   (5-ounce) skinless chicken thighs

 3   slices turkey bacon, cut into ¼-inch slices

 ½   cup dry white wine

♦ ½   cup low-sodium chicken broth

 ¼   teaspoon salt

 ¼   teaspoon black pepper

 3   ounces turkey kielbasa, halved lengthwise and sliced (¾ cup)

♦ 1   (19-ounce) can cannellini (white kidney) beans, rinsed and drained

1 Combine carrots, leek, garlic, and herbes de Provence in 5- or 6-quart slow cooker.

2 Spray large nonstick skillet with nonstick spray and set over medium-high heat. Add chicken and cook until browned, about 4 minutes. Turn chicken and sprinkle bacon around it; cook, stirring bacon occasionally, until chicken and bacon are browned, about 4 minutes.

3 Transfer chicken and bacon to slow cooker. Add wine, broth, salt, and pepper to skillet; bring to boil, scraping up browned bits from bottom of pan. Pour broth mixture over chicken. Top with kielbasa and beans. Cover and cook until chicken and vegetables are fork-tender, 3–4 hours on high or 6–8 hours on low.

4 At end of cooking time, transfer chicken with slotted spoon to plate and let stand until cool enough to handle, about 15 minutes. Remove and discard bones from chicken; cut chicken into bite-size pieces. Stir chicken into slow cooker. Cover and cook on high until chicken is hot, about 2 minutes.

IN THE KITCHEN

If leeks aren't readily available, switch to 1 small finely chopped red onion.

PER SERVING (about 1½ cups): 242 Cal, 7 g Fat, 2 g Sat Fat, 0 g Trans Fat, 42 mg Chol, 651 mg Sod, 23 g Carb, 5 g Fib, 21 g Prot, 98 mg Calc.
POINTS value: *5.*

Chicken and Herb Dumpling Stew

prep 25 min • slow-cook 3 hrs • serves 4

- ◆ $3/4$ pound skinless, boneless chicken thighs, cut into $3/4$-inch chunks
- ◆ 3 large carrots, sliced
- ◆ $1/2$ pound red potatoes, scrubbed and diced
- $1/4$ teaspoon salt
- $1/4$ teaspoon black pepper
- ◆ 1 ($14^1/2$-ounce) can seasoned chicken broth with vegetables and herbs
- $1^1/2$ tablespoons water
- 1 tablespoon cornstarch
- ◆ $1^1/2$ cups frozen pearl onions, thawed
- ◆ 1 cup frozen peas, thawed
- 1 cup low-fat buttermilk baking mix
- 1 tablespoon chopped fresh dill
- ◆ 5 tablespoons fat-free milk

1 Combine chicken, carrots, potatoes, salt, and pepper in 5- or 6-quart slow cooker. Pour in broth. Press chicken mixture down into broth. Cover and cook until chicken and vegetables are fork-tender, 3–4 hours on high or 6–8 hours on low.

2 About 50 minutes before cooking time is up, whisk water and cornstarch in small bowl until smooth. Stir cornstarch mixture, onions, and peas into slow cooker. Cover and cook on high until mixture simmers and thickens, about 15 minutes.

3 Meanwhile, combine baking mix and dill in medium bowl. Stir in milk just until soft dough forms.

4 Drop dough by rounded 2 tablespoonfuls onto simmering stew, making 4 dumplings. Cover and cook until toothpick inserted into center of dumpling comes out clean, about 30 minutes.

PER SERVING (about $1^1/2$ cups stew with 1 dumpling): 373 Cal, 9 g Fat, 2 g Sat Fat, 0 g Trans Fat, 53 mg Chol, 1,001 mg Sod, 49 g Carb, 6 g Fib, 24 g Prot, 206 mg Calc. *POINTS* value: 7.

Chipotle Chicken Chili

prep 25 min • **cook/slow-cook** 4 hrs 10 min • **serves** 6

- ♦ 1 pound skinless, boneless chicken thighs, cut into $1/2$-inch cubes
- 2 tablespoons + 1 teaspoon chipotle chile powder
- ♦ 1 large red onion, chopped
- ♦ 2 large red bell peppers, diced
- ♦ 1 ($14^1/2$-ounce) can diced tomatoes in sauce
- Juice of 1 orange
- 1 tablespoon packed brown sugar
- 2 teaspoons ground cumin
- 1 bay leaf
- $1^1/2$ teaspoons unsweetened cocoa
- $1/2$ teaspoon instant espresso powder
- ♦ 1 (9-ounce) box frozen corn kernels, thawed
- ♦ 2 tablespoons cornmeal
- $1/3$ cup chopped pistachios

1 Spray large nonstick skillet with nonstick spray and set over medium-high heat. Add half of chicken and $1/2$ teaspoon chile powder; cook, stirring occasionally, until browned, about 5 minutes. Transfer chicken mixture to 5- or 6-quart slow cooker. Repeat with remaining chicken and $1/2$ teaspoon chile powder.

2 Add remaining 2 tablespoons chile powder, onion, bell peppers, tomatoes, orange juice, brown sugar, cumin, bay leaf, cocoa, and espresso powder to slow cooker; mix well. Press chicken and vegetables down so they form even layer. Top with corn, leaving $1/2$-inch border from side of slow cooker. Cover and cook until chicken and vegetables are fork-tender, 4–5 hours on high or 8–10 hours on low.

3 About 20 minutes before cooking time is up, gradually stir cornmeal into slow cooker until blended. Cover and cook on high until mixture simmers and thickens, 15 minutes. Serve, sprinkled with pistachios.

♦ **FILLING EXTRA**
Try this recipe with 1 (12-ounce) bag thawed frozen corn kernels instead of the 9-ounce box.

PER SERVING (about $3/4$ cup): 287 Cal, 11 g Fat, 3 g Sat Fat, 0 g Trans Fat, 51 mg Chol, 223 mg Sod, 33 g Carb, 7 g Fib, 19 g Prot, 65 mg Calc.
POINTS value: *6.*

Osso Buco–Style Drumsticks

prep 25 min · **slow-cook** 3 hrs · **serves** 4

- 1 (14½-ounce) can diced tomatoes with roasted garlic and onions
- 4 carrots, chopped
- 2 stalks celery, chopped
- ¼ cup red wine
- 2 tablespoons chopped sun-dried tomatoes (not oil-packed)
- 1 teaspoon Italian seasoning
- ¼ teaspoon red pepper flakes
- ¼ teaspoon salt
- 8 (¼-pound) skinless chicken drumsticks
- ¼ cup plain dried bread crumbs

TOPPING

- 3 tablespoons chopped fresh parsley
- Grated zest of ½ lemon

1 Combine canned tomatoes, carrots, celery, wine, sun-dried tomatoes, Italian seasoning, red pepper flakes, and salt in 5- or 6-quart slow cooker. Add chicken. Press chicken down into tomato mixture. Cover and cook until chicken and vegetables are fork-tender, 3–4 hours on high or 6–8 hours on low.

2 About 20 minutes before cooking time is up, gradually stir bread crumbs into slow cooker until blended. Cover and cook on high until mixture simmers and thickens, about 15 minutes.

3 Meanwhile, to make topping, combine parsley and lemon zest in bowl. Divide stew evenly among 4 plates. Serve, sprinkled with topping.

◆ FILLING EXTRA

For an additional **1 POINTS** value per serving, prepare the recipe as directed, but after adding the bread crumbs in step 2, stir in 2 cups thawed frozen baby lima beans.

PER SERVING (2 chicken drumsticks with 1 cup vegetables and sauce and about 2 teaspoons topping): 223 Cal, 5 g Fat, 1 g Sat Fat, 0 g Trans Fat, 97 mg Chol, 509 mg Sod, 17 g Carb, 4 g Fib, 28 g Prot, 107 mg Calc. *POINTS* value: *4.*

Meatball Heroes

1½ cups fat-free marinara sauce

4 tablespoons plain dried bread crumbs

♦ 1 pound ground skinless chicken or turkey breast

1 shallot, minced

¼ cup chopped fresh parsley

¾ teaspoon Italian seasoning

¼ teaspoon black pepper

3 tablespoons low-fat (1%) milk or water

3 tablespoons grated pecorino cheese

1 (½-pound) multigrain baguette, split

1 Mix marinara sauce and 1 tablespoon bread crumbs in 5- or 6-quart slow cooker.

2 Combine chicken, shallot, parsley, Italian seasoning, pepper, milk, pecorino, and remaining 3 tablespoons bread crumbs in large bowl. With moistened hands, form into 12 meatballs.

3 Add meatballs, a few at a time, to slow cooker. Cover and cook until instant-read thermometer inserted into center of meatball registers 170°F, 3–4 hours on high or 6–8 hours on low.

4 At end of cooking time, cut baguette crosswise into 8 equal pieces. Spoon 3 meatballs and 2 tablespoons sauce onto bottom half of each piece. Cover with top halves of baguette. Serve with remaining sauce.

♦ FILLING EXTRA

Cut 1 fennel bulb into thin wedges to serve alongside the heroes.

PER SERVING (1 hero with ¼ cup sauce): 385 Cal, 7 g Fat, 2 g Sat Fat, 0 g Trans Fat, 75 mg Chol, 914 mg Sod, 43 g Carb, 4 g Fib, 37 g Prot, 164 mg Calc. *POINTS* value: **7.**

Turkey with Chili-Orange Sauce

prep 20 min • **slow-cook** 3 hrs 20 min • **serves** 4

^{1}/$_2$ cup dry white wine or low-sodium chicken broth

^{1}/$_4$ cup frozen orange juice concentrate

4 shallots, sliced

3 tablespoons low-sodium soy sauce

1 teaspoon Asian chili garlic sauce

1 teaspoon ancho chile powder

◆ 1 skinless, boneless turkey-breast half (about 1^1/$_2$ pounds)

2 tablespoons cold water

1 tablespoon cornstarch

2 tablespoons low-sugar orange marmalade

1 teaspoon white-wine vinegar

1 Combine wine, orange juice concentrate, shallots, soy sauce, chili garlic sauce, and chile powder in 5- or 6-quart slow cooker. Top with turkey. Cover and cook until turkey is fork-tender, 3–4 hours on high or 6–8 hours on low.

2 At end of cooking time, transfer turkey to cutting board; cover with foil and keep warm. Whisk water and cornstarch in small bowl until smooth. Stir cornstarch mixture into slow cooker. Cover and cook on high until mixture simmers and thickens, about 20 minutes. Stir in marmalade and vinegar.

3 Cut turkey into 12 slices and serve with sauce.

PER SERVING (3 slices turkey with about ^{1}/$_3$ cup sauce): 275 Cal, 2 g Fat, 1 g Sat Fat, 0 g Trans Fat, 114 mg Chol, 504 mg Sod, 20 g Carb, 1 g Fib, 42 g Prot, 42 mg Calc. *POINTS* value: *5.*

Mexicali Turkey Breast

prep 30 min • **slow-cook** 3 hrs 20 min • **serves** 4

1	tablespoon smoked paprika
1	teaspoon chili powder
1	teaspoon dried thyme, crumbled
1/4	teaspoon salt
♦ 1	small red onion, finely chopped
♦ 1	cup mild chunky fat-free salsa
♦ 1	skinless, boneless turkey-breast half (about 1 1/2 pounds)
1	teaspoon olive oil
♦ 3	poblano peppers, coarsely chopped
♦ 1 1/2	tablespoons cornmeal
♦ 1	cup frozen corn kernels, thawed
1	teaspoon balsamic vinegar

1 Mix paprika, chili powder, thyme, and salt in cup. Combine onion, salsa, and 1 tablespoon paprika mixture in 5- or 6-quart slow cooker. Rub all sides of turkey with oil, then remaining paprika mixture.

2 Transfer turkey to slow cooker. Place poblanos around both sides of turkey. Cover and cook until turkey and vegetables are fork-tender, 3–4 hours on high or 6–8 hours on low.

3 At end of cooking time, transfer turkey to cutting board; cover with foil and keep warm. Gradually stir cornmeal into slow cooker until blended. Stir in corn. Cover and cook on high until mixture simmers and thickens and corn is just tender, about 20 minutes. Stir in vinegar.

4 Cut turkey into 12 slices. Serve with vegetables and sauce.

This recipe works with the Simply Filling technique.

PER SERVING (3 slices turkey with 3/4 cup vegetables and sauce): 285 Cal, 4 g Fat, 1 g Sat Fat, 0 g Trans Fat, 114 mg Chol, 621 mg Sod, 20 g Carb, 4 g Fib, 43 g Prot, 59 mg Calc. *POINTS* value: *5.*

Sicilian Turkey Roll

prep 40 min · **cook/slow-cook** 3 hrs 10 min · **serves** 4

- 1 large onion, chopped
- 1/2 cup dry white wine or low-sodium chicken broth
- 1/2 teaspoon salt
- 1 teaspoon olive oil
- 2 cups chopped fresh Swiss chard leaves
- 2 garlic cloves, finely chopped
- 3 tablespoons raisins, chopped
- 1/2 teaspoon dried marjoram
- 1 skinless, boneless turkey breast half (about 1 1/2 pounds)
- 1/4 teaspoon black pepper
- 4 (1/2-ounce) slices prosciutto or baked ham
- 3 tablespoons grated pecorino cheese

1 Set aside 3/4 cup chopped onion for filling. Mix remaining chopped onion, wine, and 1/4 teaspoon salt in 5- or 6-quart slow cooker.

2 Heat oil in large nonstick skillet over medium heat. Add reserved 3/4 cup chopped onion and cook until softened, about 5 minutes. Add Swiss chard and garlic; cook, stirring occasionally, until vegetables are tender and liquid has evaporated, about 3 minutes. Stir in raisins and marjoram. Remove skillet from heat and let filling cool slightly, about 10 minutes.

3 Place turkey, skinned side up, on cutting board. Holding sharp knife parallel to board and starting at one long side, cut three quarters of way through and open up half breast like a book. Cover with sheet of plastic wrap. With meat mallet or rolling pin, gently pound to 1/2-inch thickness. Sprinkle with remaining 1/4 teaspoon salt and pepper. Lay prosciutto onto turkey leaving 1/2-inch border. Spread filling evenly over prosciutto, then sprinkle with pecorino. Starting at one narrow end, roll up jelly-roll fashion. Tie with kitchen string at 1-inch intervals.

4 Transfer roll to slow cooker. Cover and cook until turkey is fork-tender, 3–4 hours on high or 6–8 hours on low. Transfer roll to cutting board. Remove string and cut into 12 slices. Serve with sauce.

PER SERVING (3 slices turkey with 5 tablespoons sauce): 290 Cal, 6 g Fat, 2 g Sat Fat, 0 g Trans Fat, 127 mg Chol, 585 mg Sod, 11 g Carb, 2 g Fib, 46 g Prot, 108 mg Calc. *POINTS* value: **6.**

Hot-and-Spicy Turkey Curry

prep 15 min • **slow-cook** 4 hrs • **serves** 4

- ◆ 1   red onion, sliced
- ◆ ³/₄   pound Yukon Gold potatoes, scrubbed and cut into 1-inch chunks
- ◆ 1   pound turkey cutlets, cut into 1-inch chunks
- ½   teaspoon salt
- ◆ 1½ cups low-sodium chicken broth
- 2   teaspoons Thai green curry paste
- 2   teaspoons curry powder
- ◆ 1   (16-ounce) bag frozen broccoli, thawed
- ½   cup light coconut milk
- 2   tablespoons chopped fresh cilantro

1 In single layers, place onion, potatoes, and turkey in 5- or 6-quart slow cooker. Sprinkle with salt. Mix broth, curry paste, and curry powder in bowl; pour over chicken and vegetables. Cover and cook until chicken and vegetables are fork-tender, 4–5 hours on high or 8–10 hours on low.

2 About 25 minutes before cooking time is up, stir broccoli and coconut milk into slow cooker. Cover and cook on high until broccoli is crisp-tender, about 20 minutes. Serve, sprinkled with cilantro.

◆ **FILLING EXTRA**
Serve this saucy curry with 2 cups cooked bulgur (½ cup cooked bulgur for each serving will increase the **POINTS** value by **1**).

PER SERVING (1³/₄ cups): 260 Cal, 5 g Fat, 2 g Sat Fat, 0 g Trans Fat, 64 mg Chol, 489 mg Sod, 26 g Carb, 5 g Fib, 5 g Prot, 56 mg Calc. *POINTS* value: *5.*

Spicy Asian Turkey

prep 20 min • **slow-cook** 3 hrs 20 min • **serves** 6

◆ 1   (1-pound) bag baby carrots

1/4   **cup Thai sweet red chili sauce**

2   **tablespoons thin strips peeled fresh ginger**

2   **tablespoons rice-wine vinegar**

1   **tablespoon low-sodium soy sauce**

◆ 2   (1-pound) turkey thighs, skinned

2   **tablespoons cold water**

1   **tablespoon cornstarch**

◆ 1   (15-ounce) can baby corn, drained

◆ 2   cups frozen sugar-snap peas, thawed

1/4   **cup chopped fresh cilantro**

1 Combine carrots, chili sauce, ginger, vinegar, and soy sauce in 5- or 6-quart slow cooker. Top with turkey. Cover and cook until turkey and carrots are fork-tender, 3–4 hours on high or 6–8 hours on low.

2 At end of cooking time, transfer turkey with slotted spoon to plate and let stand until cool enough to handle, about 20 minutes.

3 Meanwhile, whisk water and cornstarch in small bowl until smooth; stir in about 1/4 cup hot liquid from slow cooker until blended. Stir cornstarch mixture into slow cooker. Stir in corn and snap peas. Cover and cook on high until mixture simmers and thickens and snap peas are crisp-tender, about 20 minutes.

4 Remove and discard bones from turkey; cut turkey into bite-size pieces. Stir turkey into slow cooker. Cover and cook on high until turkey is hot, about 2 minutes. Serve, sprinkled with cilantro.

PER SERVING (about $1^1/_2$ cups): 251 Cal, 5 g Fat, 1 g Sat Fat, 0 g Trans Fat, 94 mg Chol, 545 mg Sod, 25 g Carb, 5 g Fib, 28 g Prot, 78 mg Calc. *POINTS* value: 5.

Turkey Picadillo

prep 15 min • **slow-cook** 3 hrs 20 min • **serves** 4

- 1 (14½-ounce) can diced tomatoes with garlic, drained
- 1 green bell pepper, chopped
- 3 tablespoons tomato paste
- 2 **tablespoons honey**
- 2 **tablespoons chili powder**
- 2 **teaspoons unsweetened cocoa**
- 1½ **teaspoons ground cumin**
- ¾ **teaspoon salt**
- 2 (1-pound) turkey thighs, skinned
- 2 tablespoons cornmeal
- 1½ cups frozen corn kernels, thawed
- 3 **tablespoons dried currants**
- 1 **tablespoon cayenne pepper sauce**

1 Combine tomatoes, bell pepper, tomato paste, honey, chili powder, cocoa, cumin, and salt in 5- or 6-quart slow cooker. Top with turkey. Cover and cook until turkey and bell pepper are fork-tender, 3–4 hours on high or 6–8 hours on low.

2 At end of cooking time, transfer turkey with slotted spoon to plate and let stand until cool enough to handle, about 20 minutes.

3 Meanwhile, gradually stir cornmeal into slow cooker until blended. Stir in corn, currants, and pepper sauce. Cover and cook on high until mixture simmers and thickens and corn is just tender, about 20 minutes.

4 Remove and discard bones from turkey; cut turkey into bite-size pieces. Ladle vegetables and sauce evenly among 4 bowls. Top evenly with turkey.

IN THE KITCHEN

For another **1 POINTS** value per serving, sprinkle this classic Latin-American dish with ¼ cup sliced almonds.

PER SERVING (¾ cup turkey with ¾ cup vegetables and sauce): 371 Cal, 7 g Fat, 2 g Sat Fat, 0 g Trans Fat, 140 mg Chol, 920 mg Sod, 40 g Carb, 6 g Fib, 41 g Prot, 99 mg Calc. **POINTS** value: 7.

Cranberry-Orange Turkey

prep 25 min • slow-cook 3 hrs 15 min • serves 4

- ♦ 1 cup fresh or thawed frozen cranberries
- ♦ 3 carrots, chopped
- 1/2 cup low-sugar orange marmalade
- 1 1/2 teaspoons ground ginger
- 1/2 teaspoon five-spice powder or apple or pumpkin pie spice
- 3/4 teaspoon salt
- ♦ 2 (3/4-pound) turkey drumsticks, skinned
- 2 tablespoons cold water
- 1 tablespoon cornstarch
- ♦ 2 cups frozen sugar-snap peas, thawed
- ♦ 2 large scallions, chopped

1 Combine cranberries, carrots, marmalade, ginger, five-spice powder, and salt in 5- or 6-quart slow cooker. Top with turkey. Cover and cook until turkey and carrots are fork-tender, 3–4 hours on high or 6–8 hours on low.

2 At end of cooking time, transfer turkey with slotted spoon to plate and let stand until cool enough to handle, about 20 minutes.

3 Meanwhile, whisk water and cornstarch in small bowl until smooth; stir in about 1/4 cup hot liquid from slow cooker until blended. Stir cornstarch mixture into slow cooker. Stir in snap peas. Cover and cook on high until mixture simmers and thickens and snap peas are crisp-tender, about 15 minutes. Stir in scallions.

4 Remove and discard bones from turkey; with 2 forks, shred turkey into small pieces. Ladle vegetables and sauce evenly among 4 bowls. Top evenly with turkey.

♦ FILLING EXTRA
Serve 2 cups cooked wild rice with this Thanksgiving-inspired stew (1/2 cup cooked rice per serving will increase the *POINTS* value by *1*).

PER SERVING (3/4 cup turkey with 3/4 cup vegetables and sauce): 281 Cal, 4 g Fat, 1 g Sat Fat, 0 g Trans Fat, 91 mg Chol, 545 mg Sod, 35 g Carb, 5 g Fib, 27 g Prot, 91 mg Calc. *POINTS* value: *5.*

Creamy Turkey Meatballs

prep 20 min • bake/slow-cook 1 hr 15 min • serves 4

3 slices firm white bread, torn into small pieces

♦ 1 pound ground skinless turkey breast

2 shallots, finely chopped

♦ 1 large egg

2 tablespoons whole-grain mustard

½ teaspoon salt

¼ teaspoon black pepper

¼ teaspoon ground allspice

♦ ½ cup low-sodium chicken broth

1 teaspoon steak sauce

♦ ½ cup fat-free sour cream

1 Preheat oven to 450°F. Lightly spray large rimmed baking sheet with nonstick spray.

2 Pulse bread in food processor or blender to fine crumbs. Combine bread crumbs, turkey, shallots, egg, 1 tablespoon mustard, salt, pepper, and allspice in large bowl. Form into 36 meatballs. Place meatballs on baking sheet 1 inch apart. Bake until lightly browned, about 15 minutes.

3 Transfer meatballs to 5- or 6-quart slow cooker. Mix broth, remaining 1 tablespoon mustard, and steak sauce in small bowl; pour over meatballs. Cover and cook until instant-read thermometer inserted in center of meatball registers 170°F and sauce thickens slightly, 1–2 hours on high or 2–4 hours on low.

4 At end of cooking time, stir sour cream into slow cooker.

PER SERVING (9 meatballs with 3 tablespoons sauce): 225 Cal, 3 g Fat, 0 g Sat Fat, 0 g Trans Fat, 129 mg Chol, 750 mg Sod, 15 g Carb, 0 g Fib, 33 g Prot, 87 mg Calc. *POINTS* value: *5.*

Turkey Strata

prep 35 min • cook/slow-cook 3 hrs 10 min • serves 6

$1/2$ pound sweet Italian turkey sausage links, casings removed

♦ 1 onion, chopped

♦ 1 (10-ounce) box frozen chopped broccoli, thawed and squeezed dry

$1^1/2$ teaspoons dried tarragon

5 slices day-old whole wheat bread, cubed (about 5 cups)

1 cup shredded low-fat Italian cheese blend

$2^1/2$ cups low-fat (1%) milk

♦ $1^1/2$ cups fat-free egg substitute

1 tablespoon Dijon mustard

$3/4$ teaspoon salt

$1/4$ teaspoon black pepper

1 Spray large nonstick skillet with nonstick spray and set over medium heat. Add sausage and onion; cook, breaking sausage apart with wooden spoon, until sausage is no longer pink, about 6 minutes. Add broccoli and tarragon; increase heat and cook, stirring occasionally, until broccoli is crisp-tender, about 3 minutes.

2 Spray 5- or 6-quart slow cooker stoneware with nonstick spray. In single layers, place $2^1/2$ cups bread, half sausage mixture, and $1/2$ cup cheese blend in slow cooker. Repeat with remaining $2^1/2$ cups bread, sausage mixture, and $1/2$ cup cheese blend.

3 Whisk milk, egg substitute, mustard, salt, and pepper in large bowl; pour over bread-sausage mixture. Cover and cook until knife inserted into center of strata comes out clean, 3–4 hours on low.

4 Transfer stoneware to rack and let strata cool slightly, 30 minutes. Cut strata into 6 wedges.

IN THE KITCHEN

Want to make this dish but don't have day-old bread handy? Not a problem. Just lightly toast the slices, let cool, and cut into cubes.

PER SERVING (1 wedge): 270 Cal, 8 g Fat, 3 g Sat Fat, 0 g Trans Fat, 47 mg Chol, 1,019 mg Sod, 21 g Carb, 4 g Fib, 29 g Prot, 414 mg Calc. POINTS value: 5.

Vietnamese Cornish Hens

prep 20 min • **slow-cook/cook** 3 hrs 10 min • **serves** 4

- ♦ 1/2 large butternut squash, peeled and cut into 3/4-inch slices
- ♦ 1 onion, quartered and thinly sliced
- ♦ 2 (1 1/2-pound) Cornish hens, halved and skinned
- 1 lime
- 3 tablespoons packed brown sugar
- 2 teaspoons Asian fish sauce
- 1 teaspoon Sriracha (hot chili sauce) or cayenne pepper sauce
- 3/4 teaspoon ground ginger

1 Combine squash and onion in 5- or 6-quart slow cooker. Top with hens so backbones face toward edge of slow cooker.

2 Grate zest from lime; cut lime into 4 wedges. Combine lime zest, brown sugar, fish sauce, chili sauce, and ginger in small bowl; spoon evenly over hens. Cover and cook until hens and vegetables are fork-tender, 3–4 hours on high or 6–8 hours on low.

3 Transfer hens and vegetables with slotted spoon to serving platter; cover with foil and keep warm. Transfer cooking liquid to medium skillet and bring to boil. Boil until mixture is syrupy glaze and reduced to about 1/3 cup, about 7 minutes. Serve with hens and lime wedges.

PER SERVING (1/2 hen with 3/4 cup vegetables and 4 teaspoons glaze): 325 Cal, 7 g Fat, 2 g Sat Fat, 0 g Trans Fat, 179 mg Chol, 366 mg Sod, 26 g Carb, 3 g Fib, 41 g Prot, 85 mg Calc. *POINTS* value: *6.*

Cornish Hens with Fines Herbes

prep 20 min • **slow-cook/cook** 3 hrs 5 min • **serves** 4

1 tablespoon each chopped fresh parsley, tarragon, chervil, and chives

5 teaspoons unsalted butter, softened

3/4 teaspoon salt

1/4 teaspoon black pepper

◆ 2 (1 1/2-pound) Cornish hens

◆ 3/4 cup low-sodium chicken broth

2 tablespoons quick-cooking tapioca

1/8 teaspoon ground mace or nutmeg

1/4 cup fat-free half-and-half

1 Combine parsley, tarragon, chervil, and chives in cup. Transfer 1 tablespoon herb mixture to another cup; cover and refrigerate. Mash remaining 3 tablespoons herb mixture, butter, 1/2 teaspoon salt, and 1/8 teaspoon pepper with wooden spoon in small bowl until blended. With fingertips, gently separate skin from meat on breasts, thighs, and legs of hens. Pat meat dry with paper towels. Spread butter mixture evenly on meat under skin. Transfer hens to 5- or 6-quart slow cooker.

2 Mix broth, tapioca, mace, and remaining 1/4 teaspoon salt and 1/8 teaspoon pepper in bowl. Pour broth mixture over hens. Cover and cook until hens are fork-tender, 3–4 hours on high or 6–8 hours on low.

3 Transfer hens to cutting board; cover with foil and keep warm. Strain sauce through sieve into small saucepan, pressing solids through sieve with rubber spatula. Bring sauce to boil; stir in reserved 1 tablespoon herb mixture and half-and-half. Remove saucepan from heat.

4 Remove skin from hens; cut each in half. Serve with sauce.

IN THE KITCHEN
Fines herbes is a delicious combination of parsley, tarragon, chervil, and chives often used in French cooking. But you can simplify this dish by substituting 1/4 cup chopped fresh tarragon.

PER SERVING (1/2 hen with 1/3 cup sauce): 263 Cal, 10 g Fat, 4 g Sat Fat, 0 g Trans Fat, 159 mg Chol, 653 mg Sod, 7 g Carb, 0 g Fib, 33 g Prot, 51 mg Calc. *POINTS* value: **6.**

Smoky Duck Chili

prep 25 min · cook/slow-cook 4 hrs 10 min · serves 6

- 1 pound skinless, boneless duck breasts, cut into $1/2$-inch cubes

Grated zest and juice of 1 orange

- 6 carrots, sliced
- 1 red onion, sliced
- 1 ($14^1/_2$-ounce) can diced tomatoes with roasted garlic
- 1 (8-ounce) can tomato sauce (no salt added)
- 1 (15-ounce) can black beans, rinsed and drained

2 tablespoons chipotle chile powder

1 tablespoon chopped fresh rosemary or 1 teaspoon dried

1 teaspoon ground coriander

$1/4$ cup chopped fresh cilantro

1 Spray large nonstick skillet with nonstick spray and set over medium-high heat. Add half of duck and cook, turning occasionally, until browned, about 4 minutes. Transfer duck to 5- or 6-quart slow cooker. Repeat with remaining duck.

2 Add orange juice to skillet. Bring to boil, scraping up browned bits from bottom of pan. Pour orange juice mixture into slow cooker. Stir in carrots, onion, diced tomatoes, tomato sauce, beans, orange zest, chile powder, rosemary, and coriander. Cover and cook until duck and vegetables are fork-tender, 4–5 hours on high or 8–10 hours on low. Serve, sprinkled with cilantro.

IN THE KITCHEN
Chipotle chile powder is readily available in the spice aisle at the supermarket. It's made from smoked dried jalapeño peppers, giving this dish a rich complex flavor.

PER SERVING (about 1 cup): 318 Cal, 5 g Fat, 1 g Sat Fat, 0 g Trans Fat, 81 mg Chol, 589 mg Sod, 50 g Carb, 11 g Fib, 23 g Prot, 151 mg Calc.
POINTS value: *6.*

Fruited Duck Stew

prep 25 min • **cook/slow-cook** 4 hrs 35 min • **serves** 6

- 2½ pounds skinless, boneless duck breasts
- 2½ pounds whole duck legs, skinned
- ½ teaspoon salt
- ½ teaspoon black pepper
- 1 onion, sliced
- 1 (16-ounce) bag shredded red cabbage
- 1 cup red wine
- 1 tablespoon chopped fresh thyme or 1 teaspoon dried
- 1 cup low-sodium chicken broth
- ½ cup dried cranberries
- ⅓ cup dried peaches or apricots, thinly sliced
- 3 tablespoons balsamic vinegar
- 1 tablespoon honey
- 2 teaspoons cornstarch

1 Sprinkle duck with salt and pepper. Heat large nonstick skillet over medium-high heat. Add half of duck and cook until browned, about 5 minutes per side. Transfer duck to 5- or 6-quart slow cooker. Repeat with remaining duck.

2 Add onion to skillet. Reduce heat and cook, stirring occasionally, until browned, about 5 minutes. Remove skillet from heat; stir in cabbage, wine, and thyme. Transfer cabbage mixture to slow cooker; stir in broth, cranberries, and peaches. Cover and cook until duck and vegetables are fork-tender, 4–5 hours on high or 8–10 hours on low.

3 At end of cooking time, transfer duck with slotted spoon to cutting board and let stand until cool enough to handle, about 15 minutes. Whisk vinegar, honey, and cornstarch in small bowl until smooth; stir in about ¼ cup hot liquid from slow cooker until blended. Stir cornstarch mixture into slow cooker. Cover and cook on high until mixture simmers and thickens, about 10 minutes.

4 Remove and discard bones from duck legs; cut leg and breast meat into 1½-inch pieces. Stir duck into slow cooker. Cover and let stand until duck is heated through, about 5 minutes.

PER SERVING (about 1 cup): 360 Cal, 4 g Fat, 1 g Sat Fat, 0 g Trans Fat, 153 mg Chol, 337 mg Sod, 32 g Carb, 4 g Fib, 51 g Prot, 82 mg Calc.
POINTS value: **7.**

PORK AND TOMATILLO
STEW, PAGE 119

Chapter 4

Big Batch Winners

When a crowd is coming, a slow cooker can save you. Try these meals to serve 8 or more. Plus, we give directions for freezing and reheating.

Corned Beef with Beet Relish

prep 20 min • **slow-cook/cook** 4 hrs • **serves** 6 plus leftovers

---

◆ 1   pound leeks, cleaned and cut into 2-inch pieces, white and light green parts only

   3   garlic cloves, chopped

   1   (3-pound) lean corned beef brisket, trimmed

◆ 1¹/₂   pounds red potatoes, scrubbed and cut into 2-inch chunks

◆ 1   cup baby carrots

◆ ¹/₂   head Savoy cabbage, cut into 8 wedges

◆ 1¹/₂   cups low-sodium chicken broth

◆ 1   pound beets, trimmed

  ¹/₄   cup prepared horseradish

   1   tablespoon cider vinegar

   1   tablespoon chopped fresh dill

  ¹/₄   teaspoon salt

1 Combine leeks and garlic in 5- or 6-quart slow cooker. Top with beef. Place potatoes and carrots around beef. Top vegetables with cabbage. Pour broth over vegetables. Cover and cook until beef and vegetables are fork-tender, 4–5 hours on high or 8–10 hours on low.

2 Meanwhile, to make relish, bring beets and enough cold water to cover to boil in large saucepan. Reduce heat; partially cover and simmer until fork-tender, 45–50 minutes. Drain and let cool. Peel and coarsely chop. Put beets, horseradish, vinegar, dill, and salt in food processor and pulse until finely chopped.

3 Transfer beef to cutting board and cut crosswise into 2 pieces. Transfer half of beef to freezer container. Top with half of vegetables (about 3 cups) and 1 cup cooking liquid and let cool. Cover and freeze up to 2 months. Transfer half of relish (³/₄ cup) to another airtight container. Cover and refrigerate up to 1 week (serve with grilled beef, pork, or chicken). Discard remaining cooking liquid. Cut remaining piece of beef across grain into 12 slices. Serve with remaining 3 cups vegetables and ³/₄ cup relish.

TO REHEAT
Thaw the beef, vegetables, and cooking liquid in the refrigerator overnight. Transfer to a Dutch oven. Cover and cook over medium heat, stirring occasionally, until heated through, 25–30 minutes. Discard the cooking liquid before serving.

PER SERVING (2 slices beef with ¹/₂ cup vegetables and 2 tablespoons relish): 187 Cal, 8 g Fat, 3 g Sat Fat, 0 g Trans Fat, 39 mg Chol, 574 mg Sod, 19 g Carb, 4 g Fib, 10 g Prot, 51 mg Calc. *POINTS* value: *4.*

Roast Beef with Tomatoes and Mushrooms

prep 20 min • cook/slow-cook 4 hrs 30 min • serves 4 plus leftovers

- 1 (2½-pound) eye-round roast, trimmed
- 1 teaspoon salt
- ½ teaspoon black pepper
- 1 teaspoon olive oil
- 2 red onions, sliced
- 1 (10-ounce) package sliced cremini mushrooms
- 2 shallots, finely chopped
- 1 tablespoon chopped fresh oregano or 1 teaspoon dried
- 1 (28-ounce) can fire-roasted tomatoes, chopped
- ½ cup low-sodium beef broth

1 Sprinkle beef with ½ teaspoon salt and ¼ teaspoon pepper. Heat oil in large nonstick skillet over medium-high heat. Add beef and cook, turning frequently, until browned, about 6 minutes. Transfer beef with tongs to 5- or 6-quart slow cooker.

2 Add onions, mushrooms, shallots, and oregano to skillet. Reduce heat and cook, stirring occasionally, until vegetables are softened, 6–7 minutes. Add tomatoes, broth, remaining ½ teaspoon salt and ¼ teaspoon pepper; cook, stirring occasionally, until mixture slightly thickens, 5–6 minutes. Pour tomato mixture over beef. Cover and cook until beef is fork-tender, 4–5 hours on high or 8–10 hours on low.

3 Transfer beef to cutting board; cover with foil and keep warm. Pour sauce into large saucepan; bring to boil over medium-high heat. Boil, stirring occasionally, until slightly thickened and reduced by about one third, 15–18 minutes.

4 Cut beef crosswise into 2 pieces. Transfer half of beef to freezer container. Top with half of sauce and vegetables (about 2 cups) and let cool. Cover and freeze up to 2 months. Cut remaining piece of beef into 8 slices. Serve with remaining 2 cups sauce and vegetables.

TO REHEAT

Thaw the beef, and the sauce and vegetable mixture in the refrigerator overnight. Transfer to a small baking dish; cover with foil. Bake in a 350°F oven until heated through, about 25 minutes.
This recipe works with the Simply Filling Technique.

PER SERVING: (2 slices beef with about ½ cup sauce and vegetables)
273 Cal, 6 g Fat, 2 g Sat Fat, 0 g Trans Fat, 101 mg Chol, 496 mg Sod,
9 g Carb, 2 g Fib, 43 g Prot, 54 mg Calc. *POINTS* value: *6.*

Wild Mushroom Steak Roulades

prep 30 min • cook/slow-cook 4 hrs 10 min • serves 4 plus leftovers

4	teaspoons olive oil
♦ 1	pound shiitake mushrooms, stems removed and sliced
♦ 1	(10-ounce) package sliced cremini mushrooms
♦ 1	onion, finely chopped
2	garlic cloves, minced
3/4	teaspoon salt
1/4	cup Italian-seasoned dried bread crumbs
2	tablespoons chopped fresh thyme
♦ 2	(1-pound) flank steaks, trimmed
♦ 1/2	cup low-sodium beef broth
1/2	cup red wine
2	tablespoons water
1	tablespoon all-purpose flour

1 To make filling, heat 2 teaspoons oil in large nonstick skillet over medium-high heat. Add mushrooms, onion, garlic, and 1/4 teaspoon salt; cook, stirring occasionally, until liquid is absorbed and vegetables are very tender, 6–8 minutes. Remove skillet from heat; stir in bread crumbs and 1 tablespoon thyme. Transfer to medium bowl and let cool.

2 Place 1 steak on cutting board. Holding knife parallel to board and starting at one long side, cut three quarters of way through and open up steak like a book. Spoon half of filling over steak leaving 1/2-inch border. Starting at one narrow end, roll up jelly-roll fashion. Tie with kitchen string at 1-inch intervals. Repeat. Sprinkle with remaining 1/2 teaspoon salt.

3 Heat remaining 2 teaspoons oil in large nonstick skillet over medium-high heat. Add roulades and cook, turning, until browned, 5 minutes. Add broth, wine, and remaining 1 tablespoon thyme; bring to boil. Transfer roulades to 5- or 6-quart slow cooker. Pour in broth mixture. Cover and cook until roulades are fork-tender, 4–5 hours on high or 8–10 hours on low.

4 About 25 minutes before cooking time is up, whisk water and flour in small bowl until smooth; stir in about 1/4 cup hot liquid from slow cooker until blended. Stir flour mixture into slow cooker. Cover and cook on high until mixture simmers and thickens, about 20 minutes.

5 Transfer 1 roulade and half of sauce (about 1/2 cup) to freezer container and let cool. Cover and freeze up to 2 months. Cut remaining roulade into 8 slices and serve with remaining 1/2 cup sauce.

TO REHEAT

Thaw the roulade and sauce in the refrigerator overnight. Transfer to a small baking dish; cover with foil. Bake in a 350°F oven until heated through, 25–30 minutes.

PER SERVING (2 slices with 2 tablespoons sauce): 264 Cal, 7 g Fat, 2 g Sat Fat, 0 g Trans Fat, 83 mg Chol, 296 mg Sod, 11 g Carb, 2 g Fib, 36 g Prot, 33 mg Calc. *POINTS* value: *5.*

Italian Steak Rolls

prep 25 min • **cook/slow-cook** 4 hrs 5 min • **serves** 4 plus leftovers

....

¼ cup Italian-seasoned dried bread crumbs

¼ cup chopped fresh parsley

¼ cup grated Parmesan cheese

♦ 1 large hard-cooked egg, coarsely chopped

2 garlic cloves, minced

½ teaspoon olive oil

♦ 8 (¼-inch-thick) slices top round steak, trimmed (2 ounces each)

½ teaspoon salt

4 (3-ounce) sweet Italian turkey sausage links

1 (25-ounce) jar marinara sauce

½ cup red wine or low-sodium beef broth

¼ teaspoon red pepper flakes

1 To make filling, combine bread crumbs, parsley, Parmesan, egg, garlic, and oil in medium bowl.

2 Place 1 steak between 2 pieces of wax paper. Pound steak to ⅛-inch thickness. Repeat with remaining steaks. Remove and discard top sheets of wax paper. Press about 2 tablespoons filling onto each steak, leaving ½-inch border. From one short end, roll up each steak jelly-roll fashion. Tie each roll at 1-inch intervals with kitchen string. Sprinkle rolls with salt.

3 Spray large nonstick skillet with nonstick spray and set over medium-high heat. Add rolls and cook, turning occasionally, until browned, 3–4 minutes. Transfer rolls to 5- or 6-quart slow cooker. Add sausages to skillet and cook, turning occasionally, until browned, 3–4 minutes. Transfer sausages to slow cooker. Combine marinara sauce, wine, and red pepper flakes in large bowl; pour over rolls and sausages. Cover and cook until rolls and sausages are fork-tender, 4–5 hours on high or 8–10 hours on low.

4 Transfer 4 rolls and 2 sausages with slotted spoon to freezer container. Top with half of sauce (about 1¾ cups) and let cool. Cover and freeze up to 2 months. Remove strings from remaining 4 rolls and cut remaining 2 sausages in half. Serve with remaining 1¾ cups sauce.

TO REHEAT
Thaw the steak rolls, sausages, and sauce in the refrigerator overnight. Transfer to a saucepan. Cover and cook over medium heat, stirring occasionally, until heated through, 15–20 minutes. Remove strings from rolls and cut sausages in half.

....

PER SERVING (1 roll with ½ sausage and scant ½ cup sauce): 286 Cal, 11 g Fat, 3 g Sat Fat, 0 g Trans Fat, 99 mg Chol, 969 mg Sod, 20 g Carb, 2 g Fib, 26 g Prot, 93 mg Calc. **POINTS** value: **6.**

Smoky BBQ Beef Chili

prep 20 min • **cook/slow-cook** 4 hrs 5 min • **serves** 4 plus leftovers

1	teaspoon canola oil
◆ 1	pound ground extra-lean beef (5% fat or less)
◆ 1	onion, chopped
◆ 1	green bell pepper, chopped
3	garlic cloves, minced
◆ 1	small butternut squash, peeled and cubed
◆ 2	(15-ounce) cans pinto beans, rinsed and drained
◆ 2	cups low-sodium chicken broth
◆ 1	(14$^1/_2$-ounce) can diced tomatoes
$^2/_3$	cup chipotle barbecue sauce
$^1/_2$	teaspoon salt
2	tablespoons chopped fresh cilantro
$^1/_2$	cup shredded low-fat Cheddar cheese

1 Heat oil in large nonstick skillet over medium-high heat. Add beef, onion, bell pepper, and garlic. Brown beef, breaking it apart with wooden spoon, 6–8 minutes. Transfer beef mixture to 5- or 6-quart slow cooker. Stir in squash, beans, broth, tomatoes, barbecue sauce, and salt. Cover and cook until vegetables are fork-tender, 4–5 hours on high or 8–10 hours on low.

2 Transfer half of chili (about 5 cups) to freezer container and let cool. Cover and freeze up to 3 months. Stir cilantro into remaining 5 cups chili. Serve, sprinkled with Cheddar.

TO REHEAT
Thaw the chili in the refrigerator overnight. Transfer to a saucepan. Cover and cook over medium heat, stirring occasionally, until heated through, 12–15 minutes.

PER SERVING (1$^1/_4$ cups chili with 2 tablespoons cheese): 295 Cal, 9 g Fat, 4 g Sat Fat, 0 g Trans Fat, 45 mg Chol, 698 mg Sod, 32 g Carb, 8 g Fib, 24 g Prot, 157 mg Calc. *POINTS* value: **6.**

Zesty Pork Fajitas

prep 25 min • **cook/slow-cook** 4 hrs 15 min • **serves** 4 plus leftovers

- ◆ 1 (1³/₄-pound) boneless pork loin roast, trimmed
- ½ teaspoon salt
- ◆ 1 pound fresh tomatillos, husked, fruit rinsed, and cut into wedges
- ◆ 1 onion, sliced
- ◆ 1 (16-ounce) jar fat-free green salsa
- ◆ ½ cup low-sodium chicken broth
- ◆ 2 jalapeño peppers, seeded and chopped
- 2 garlic cloves, chopped
- ◆ 1 (15-ounce) can black beans, rinsed and drained
- ¼ cup chopped fresh cilantro
- 4 (8-inch) whole wheat tortillas
- ◆ 1 tomato, chopped

1 To make filling, sprinkle pork with salt. Spray large nonstick skillet with nonstick spray and set over medium-high heat. Add pork and cook, turning occasionally, until browned, 4–5 minutes. Transfer pork to 5- or 6-quart slow cooker. Top with tomatillos, onion, salsa, broth, jalapeños, and garlic. Cover and cook until pork and vegetables are fork-tender, 4–5 hours on high or 8–10 hours on low.

2 At end of cooking time, transfer pork with slotted spoon to plate and let cool slightly, about 10 minutes. With 2 forks, shred pork into small pieces. Stir pork, beans, and cilantro into slow cooker. Cover and cook on high until filling is heated through, about 10 minutes.

3 Transfer half of filling (about 4 cups) to freezer container and let cool. Cover and freeze up to 3 months. Spoon about 1 cup remaining filling onto each tortilla. Top tortillas evenly with tomato and fold in half.

TO REHEAT
Thaw the filling in the refrigerator overnight. Transfer to a saucepan. Cover and cook over medium heat, stirring occasionally, until heated through, 10–12 minutes.

PER SERVING (1 fajita): 356 Cal, 10 g Fat, 3 g Sat Fat, 0 g Trans Fat, 63 mg Chol, 709 mg Sod, 37 g Carb, 10 g Fib, 30 g Prot, 59 mg Calc. *POINTS* value: 7.

Apricot Pork Roast

prep 20 min • **cook/slow-cook** 4 hrs 10 min • **serves** 4 plus leftovers

◆ 1 (2½-pound) boneless pork loin roast, trimmed

1 teaspoon salt

½ teaspoon black pepper

1 teaspoon extra-virgin olive oil

◆ 1 red onion, chopped

1 tablespoon minced peeled fresh ginger

1 shallot, finely chopped

1 (12-ounce) jar apricot preserves

1 tablespoon whole-grain mustard

1 Sprinkle pork with salt and pepper. Heat oil in large nonstick skillet over medium-high heat. Add pork and cook, turning frequently, until browned, about 6 minutes. Transfer pork with tongs to 5- or 6-quart slow cooker.

2 Add onion, ginger, and shallot to skillet. Reduce heat and cook, stirring frequently, until vegetables are softened, about 2 minutes. Remove skillet from heat; stir in preserves and mustard. Pour preserves mixture over pork. Cover and cook until pork is fork-tender, 4–5 hours on high or 8–10 hours on low.

3 Transfer pork to cutting board and cut crosswise into 2 pieces. Transfer half of pork to freezer container. Top with half of sauce (about 2½ cups) and let cool. Cover and freeze up to 2 months. Cut remaining piece of pork into 8 slices. Serve with remaining 2½ cups sauce.

TO REHEAT

Thaw the pork and sauce in the refrigerator overnight. Transfer to a small baking dish; cover with foil. Bake in a 325°F oven until heated through, about 35 minutes.

PER SERVING: (2 slices pork with scant ⅔ cup sauce) 323 Cal, 10 g Fat, 4 g Sat Fat, 0 g Trans Fat, 79 mg Chol, 405 mg Sod, 30 g Carb, 0 g Fib, 28 g Prot, 35 mg Calc. *POINTS* value: 7.

Pork and Tomatillo Stew

prep 20 min • **cook/slow-cook** 4 hrs 10 min • **serves** 4 plus leftovers

- ◆ 1½ pounds fresh tomatillos, husked and fruit rinsed
- ◆ 3 poblano peppers
- ◆ 1 large onion, cut into wedges
- ◆ 2 jalapeño peppers, seeded and halved
- ◆ 1¼ pounds boneless pork loin, trimmed and cut into 1-inch cubes
-   1 teaspoon ground cumin
-   ¾ teaspoon salt
-   2 teaspoons olive oil
- ◆ 1 (15-ounce) can hominy, drained
- ◆ 1 (10-ounce) box frozen lima beans, thawed
- ◆ 1 cup low-sodium chicken broth
-   1 teaspoon dried oregano
-   2 tablespoons chopped fresh cilantro

1 Preheat broiler. Spray rimmed baking sheet with nonstick spray. Arrange tomatillos, poblanos, onion, and jalapeños on baking sheet. Broil vegetables 4 inches from heat until lightly charred, 2–3 minutes per side. Let cool slightly. Put vegetables in food processor and puree.

2 Meanwhile, sprinkle pork with cumin and salt. Heat oil in large nonstick skillet over medium-high heat. Add pork and cook, turning frequently, until browned, 5–6 minutes. Transfer pork to 5- or 6-quart slow cooker. Stir in tomatillo puree, hominy, beans, broth, and oregano. Cover and cook until pork is fork-tender, 4–5 hours on high or 8–10 hours on low.

3 Transfer half of stew (about 4 cups) to freezer container and let cool. Cover and freeze up to 2 months. Stir cilantro into remaining 4 cups stew.

TO REHEAT

Thaw the stew in the refrigerator overnight. Transfer to a saucepan. Cover and cook over medium heat, stirring occasionally, until heated through, 12–15 minutes. This recipe works with the Simply Filling technique.

PER SERVING (1 cup): 241 Cal, 8 g Fat, 2 g Sat Fat, 0 g Trans Fat, 45 mg Chol, 370 mg Sod, 22 g Carb, 6 g Fib, 21 g Prot, 38 mg Calc. *POINTS* value: *5.*

Polish Hunter's Stew

prep 25 min • cook/slow-cook 4 hrs 10 min • serves 4 plus leftovers

♦ 1 ounce dried porcini mushrooms

1 cup boiling water

♦ 1 pound pork tenderloin, trimmed and cut into 1-inch cubes

♦ 1 red onion, chopped

♦ 5 slices Canadian bacon, diced

♦ 2 pounds fresh sauerkraut, rinsed and drained

♦ 4 carrots, sliced

♦ 2 Granny Smith apples, cut into 1/2-inch slices

2 teaspoons caraway seeds

1 cup dry white wine or low-sodium chicken broth

♦ 3 tablespoons tomato paste with roasted garlic

1 pound turkey kielbasa, cut into 8 pieces

2 tablespoons chopped fresh parsley

1 Combine mushrooms and boiling water in small bowl. Let mushrooms stand until softened, about 20 minutes.

2 Meanwhile, spray large nonstick skillet with nonstick spray and set over medium-high heat. Add pork and cook, turning occasionally, until browned, about 6 minutes. Transfer pork with slotted spoon to 5- or 6-quart slow cooker. Add onion and bacon to skillet; cook, stirring occasionally, until browned, about 4 minutes. Transfer onion mixture to slow cooker. Stir in sauerkraut, carrots, apples, and caraway seeds.

3 Remove mushrooms with slotted spoon to sieve; rinse under cold water. Transfer mushrooms to cutting board and chop. Pour mushroom soaking liquid into skillet, discarding any grit in bottom of bowl. Stir in wine and tomato paste until smooth. Stir in chopped mushrooms. Pour wine mixture over pork and vegetables. Top with kielbasa. Cover and cook until pork, kielbasa, and vegetables are fork-tender, 4–5 hours on high or 8–10 hours on low.

4 Transfer half of stew (about 4 cups) and 4 pieces kielbasa to freezer container and let cool. Cover and freeze up to 2 months. Stir parsley into remaining 4 cups stew and 4 pieces kielbasa.

TO REHEAT

Thaw the stew and kielbasa in the refrigerator overnight. Transfer to a saucepan. Cover and cook over medium heat, stirring occasionally, until heated through, about 15 minutes.

PER SERVING (1 cup stew and 1 piece kielbasa): 278 Cal, 10 g Fat, 3 g Sat Fat, 0 g Trans Fat, 78 mg Chol, 1,139 mg Sod, 20 g Carb, 6 g Fib, 27 g Prot, 68 mg Calc. *POINTS* value: 6.

Slow-Cooker Cassoulet

: prep 30 min • cook/slow-cook 4 hrs 30 min • serves 4 plus leftovers

- ◆ 1/2   pound dried cannellini (white kidney) beans, picked over, rinsed, and drained
- ◆ 3   carrots, thickly sliced
- ◆ 1   red onion, coarsely chopped
- ◆ 2   large celery stalks, sliced
- 1   tablespoon salt-free garlic and herb seasoning
- 1   bay leaf
- ◆ 1   (14 1/2-ounce) can low-sodium chicken broth
- 1/4   cup water
- ◆ 2   (6-ounce) smoked bone-in center-cut pork loin chops, trimmed
- ◆ 1   (3/4-pound) boneless pork loin, cut into 1-inch cubes
- 1/2   pound fully cooked smoked chicken sausage, sliced
- ◆ 1   (14 1/2-ounce) can whole tomatoes
- 1/2   teaspoon salt
- 2   tablespoons chopped fresh parsley

1   Quick-soak beans according to package directions.

2   Combine beans, carrots, onion, celery, garlic and herb seasoning, and bay leaf in 5- or 6-quart slow cooker. Pour broth and water over top; add pork chops. Press pork chops down into bean mixture. Cover and cook until beans are tender, 4–5 hours on high or 8–10 hours on low.

3   About 1 hour before cooking time is up, spray large nonstick skillet with nonstick spray and set over medium-high heat. Add pork cubes and sausage; cook, turning occasionally, until browned, about 6 minutes. Stir in tomatoes with juice and salt, breaking tomatoes apart with wooden spoon. Transfer pork chops to plate with slotted spoon. Stir tomato mixture into slow cooker. Cover and cook on high until pork cubes are cooked through, about 45 minutes.

4   Meanwhile, let pork chops stand until cool enough to handle, about 15 minutes. Remove and discard bones from pork chops; with 2 forks, shred pork into small pieces.

5   At end of cooking time, stir shredded pork into slow cooker. Cover and let stand until pork is heated through, about 5 minutes. Transfer half of stew (about 4 cups) to freezer container and let cool. Cover and freeze up to 2 months. Serve remaining 4 cups stew sprinkled with parsley.

TO REHEAT

Thaw the stew in the refrigerator overnight. Transfer to a saucepan. Cover and cook over medium heat, stirring occasionally, until heated through, about 15 minutes.

PER SERVING (about 1 cup): 332 Cal, 13 g Fat, 4 g Sat Fat, 0 g Trans Fat, 68 mg Chol, 1,101 mg Sod, 23 g Carb, 7 g Fib, 31 g Prot, 90 mg Calc.
POINTS value: *7.*

Big Batch Winners   121

Cider Pork Chops with Sage

prep 25 min • **cook/slow-cook** 3 hrs 20 min • **serves** 4 plus leftovers

- 8 (5-ounce) bone-in pork rib chops, trimmed
- 1 tablespoon dried sage
- 3/4 teaspoon salt
- 3/4 teaspoon coarsely ground black pepper
- 2 teaspoons canola oil
- 2 onions, thinly sliced
- 4 Granny Smith apples, cut into 1/2-inch wedges
- 12 dried apricots, sliced
- 3/4 cup apple cider or unsweetened apple juice
- 3/4 cup low-sodium chicken broth
- 3/4 teaspoon cinnamon

1 Sprinkle pork chops with sage, salt, and pepper. Heat 1 teaspoon oil in large nonstick skillet over medium-high heat. Add 4 chops and cook until browned, about 2 minutes per side. Transfer to plate. Repeat with remaining 1 teaspoon oil and 4 chops.

2 Add onions to skillet. Reduce heat and cook, stirring occasionally, until golden, about 10 minutes.

3 Transfer half of onions to 5- or 6-quart slow cooker. Top with half of apples, half of apricots, and pork. Repeat with remaining onions, apples, and apricots. Combine cider, broth, and cinnamon in bowl; pour into slow cooker. Cover and cook until pork and apple mixture are fork-tender, 3–4 hours on high or 6–8 hours on low.

4 Transfer 4 chops to freezer container. Top with half of apple mixture (about 2 1/4 cups) and let cool. Cover and freeze up to 2 months. Serve remaining 4 chops with remaining 2 1/2 cups apple mixture.

TO REHEAT
Thaw the pork and apple mixture in the refrigerator overnight. Transfer to a saucepan. Cover and cook over medium heat, stirring occasionally, until heated through, 12–15 minutes.

PER SERVING (1 pork chop with generous 1/2 cup apple mixture): 249 Cal, 8 g Fat, 2 g Sat Fat, 0 g Trans Fat, 54 mg Chol, 264 mg Sod, 25 g Carb, 4 g Fib, 20 g Prot, 30 mg Calc. *POINTS* value: *5.*

Corn and Bacon Chowder

prep 15 min • cook/slow-cook 3 hrs 5 min • serves 4 plus leftovers

2   teaspoons olive oil

♦ 1   large onion, finely chopped

♦ 2   celery stalks, chopped

♦ 1   (32-ounce) carton low-sodium chicken broth

♦ 1   pound red potatoes, scrubbed and diced

2   garlic cloves, minced

1/4   cup cold water

3   tablespoons all-purpose flour

♦ 1/2   cup fat-free milk

♦ 2   cups frozen corn kernels, thawed

♦ 3   slices Canadian bacon, diced

2   tablespoons chopped fresh cilantro

1 Heat oil in large nonstick saucepan over medium-high heat. Add onion and celery; cook, stirring occasionally, until softened, 6–8 minutes. Transfer vegetables to 5- or 6-quart slow cooker. Stir in broth, potatoes, and garlic. Cover and cook until vegetables are fork-tender, 3–4 hours on high or 6–8 hours on low.

2 About 35 minutes before cooking time is up, whisk water and flour in medium bowl until smooth; whisk in milk. Stir flour mixture, corn, and bacon into slow cooker. Cover and cook on high until mixture simmers and thickens, 25–30 minutes.

3 Transfer half of chowder (about 4 cups) to freezer container and let cool. Cover and freeze up to 2 months. Stir cilantro into remaining 4 cups chowder.

TO REHEAT

Thaw the chowder in the refrigerator overnight. Transfer to a saucepan. Cover and cook over medium heat, stirring occasionally, until heated through, 10–12 minutes.

PER SERVING (1 cup): 143 Cal, 3 g Fat, 1 g Sat Fat, 0 g Trans Fat, 5 mg Chol, 175 mg Sod, 24 g Carb, 3 g Fib, 7 g Prot, 48 mg Calc. *POINTS* value: *3.*

Indian Lamb Curry

prep 30 min • **cook/slow-cook** 3 hrs 10 min • **serves** 4 plus leftovers

- 1 small red onion, coarsely chopped
- 1 (2-inch) piece peeled fresh ginger
- 1 jalapeño pepper, seeded and chopped
- 3 garlic cloves
- 1 tablespoon curry powder
- 1 teaspoon cumin seeds
- 1 teaspoon mustard seeds
- 1/2 teaspoon salt
- 1 1/2 pounds boneless leg of lamb, trimmed and cut into 1-inch cubes
- 2 teaspoons canola oil
- 1 (14 1/2-ounce) can fire-roasted diced tomatoes
- 1/2 cup low-sodium beef broth
- 2 cups frozen peas, thawed
- 3 tablespoons chopped fresh cilantro

1 Put onion, ginger, jalapeño, garlic, curry powder, cumin seeds, mustard seeds, and salt in mini–food processor and pulse until coarsely ground. Transfer mixture to large bowl. Add lamb and toss well to coat.

2 Heat 1 teaspoon oil in large nonstick skillet over medium-high heat. Add half of lamb and cook, stirring occasionally, until browned, about 5 minutes. Transfer to 5- or 6-quart slow cooker. Repeat with remaining 1 teaspoon oil and lamb. Add tomatoes and broth to skillet; cook, scraping browned bits from bottom of pan, until mixture comes to boil. Pour tomato mixture over lamb mixture. Cover and cook until lamb is fork-tender, 3–4 hours on high or 6–8 hours on low.

3 About 20 minutes before cooking time is up, stir peas into slow cooker. Cover and cook on high until peas are just tender, about 15 minutes.

4 Transfer half of curry (about 3 cups) to freezer container and let cool. Cover and freeze up to 2 months. Stir cilantro into remaining 3 cups curry.

TO REHEAT

Thaw the curry in the refrigerator overnight. Transfer to a saucepan. Cover and cook over medium heat, stirring occasionally, until heated through, 10–12 minutes. This recipe works with the Simply Filling technique.

PER SERVING (about 3/4 cup): 193 Cal, 8 g Fat, 2 g Sat Fat, 0 g Trans Fat, 59 mg Chol, 296 mg Sod, 10 g Carb, 2 g Fib, 21 g Prot, 41 mg Calc. *POINTS* value: 4.

Lamb with Stout

prep 25 min • **cook/slow-cook** 3 hrs 10 min • **serves** 4 plus leftovers

- 1¼ pounds boneless leg of lamb, trimmed and cut into 1-inch cubes
- ¾ teaspoon salt
- 1 pound small red potatoes, scrubbed and halved
- 3 carrots, cut diagonally into ½-inch slices
- 8 shallots, peeled
- 2 garlic cloves, chopped
- 2 cups low-sodium beef broth
- 1 (12-ounce) bottle stout or dark beer
- ¼ cup all-purpose flour
- ¼ cup cold water
- 1 cup frozen peas, thawed
- 2 teaspoons chopped fresh rosemary or ½ teaspoon dried

1 Sprinkle lamb with ½ teaspoon salt. Spray large nonstick skillet with nonstick spray and set over medium-high heat. Add half of lamb and cook, stirring occasionally, until browned, about 5 minutes. Transfer to 5- or 6-quart slow cooker. Repeat with remaining lamb. Top with potatoes, carrots, shallots, and garlic. Stir in broth and stout. Cover and cook until lamb and vegetables are fork-tender, 3–4 hours on high or 6–8 hours on low.

2 About 35 minutes before cooking time is up, whisk flour and water in small bowl until smooth; stir in about ¼ cup hot liquid from slow cooker until blended. Stir flour mixture into slow cooker. Cover and cook on high until mixture simmers and thickens, about 30 minutes.

3 At end of cooking time, stir peas into slow cooker. Cover and let stand until heated through, about 10 minutes.

4 Transfer half of stew (about 4 cups) to freezer container and let cool. Cover and freeze up to 2 months. Stir rosemary into remaining 4 cups stew.

TO REHEAT

Thaw the stew in the refrigerator overnight. Transfer to a saucepan. Cover and cook over medium heat, stirring occasionally, until heated through, 10–12 minutes.

PER SERVING (1 cup): 227 Cal, 5 g Fat, 2 g Sat Fat, 0 g Trans Fat, 49 mg Chol, 313 mg Sod, 24 g Carb, 3 g Fib, 19 g Prot, 44 mg Calc. *POINTS* value: *4.*

Moussaka

prep 30 min • broil/cook/slow-cook 3 hrs 30 min • serves 4 plus leftovers

◆ 1   pound eggplant, cut into
      1-inch cubes

  2   teaspoons olive oil

◆ 1   onion, finely chopped

  4   garlic cloves, minced

◆ 1 1/2 pounds lean ground lamb

◆ 1   (14 1/2-ounce) can diced
      tomatoes

  1/2 cup red wine or low-sodium
      beef broth

  1   teaspoon cinnamon

  1/2 teaspoon ground allspice

  1/2 teaspoon salt

◆ 1 3/4 cups fat-free milk

  3   tablespoons all-purpose flour

◆ 1   large egg

  1/8 teaspoon ground nutmeg

  1/2 cup grated Parmesan cheese

1 Spray broiler rack with nonstick spray; preheat broiler. Put eggplant on broiler rack and lightly spray with nonstick spray. Broil 4 inches from heat, turning occasionally, until lightly browned, about 8 minutes. Transfer to 5- or 6-quart slow cooker.

2 Meanwhile, heat oil in large nonstick skillet over medium-high heat. Add onion and garlic; cook, stirring, until onion is softened, 5–6 minutes. Add lamb and brown, 5 minutes. Stir in tomatoes, wine, cinnamon, allspice, and salt; bring to boil. Simmer, stirring, until sauce thickens slightly, 10 minutes. Spoon lamb mixture over eggplant. Cover and cook until flavors are blended, 3–4 hours on high or 6–8 hours on low.

3 To make topping, about 1 hour 10 minutes before cooking time is up, whisk milk and flour in small saucepan until smooth. Cook over medium heat, whisking constantly, until mixture boils and thickens, 3 minutes. Remove saucepan from heat. Whisk egg and nutmeg in bowl; stir in about 1/2 cup hot milk mixture. Stir egg mixture into remaining hot milk mixture until blended. Stir in Parmesan. Pour topping over eggplant mixture. Cover and cook on high just until topping is set, about 1 hour.

4 Transfer stoneware to rack and let moussaka cool slightly, about 20 minutes. Transfer half of moussaka (about 3 cups) to freezer container and let cool. Cover and freeze up to 2 months. Divide remaining 3 cups moussaka among 4 plates.

TO REHEAT

Thaw the moussaka in the refrigerator overnight. Transfer to a microwavable bowl. Cover with wax paper and microwave on High until heated through, 5–6 minutes.

PER SERVING (3/4 cup): 251 Cal, 10 g Fat, 4 g Sat Fat, 0 g Trans Fat, 91 mg Chol, 412 mg Sod, 14 g Carb, 2 g Fib, 25 g Prot, 190 mg Calc.
POINTS value: *5.*

Stuffed Breast of Veal

prep 30 min • **cook/slow-cook** 3 hrs 10 min • **serves** 4 plus leftovers

- 2 teaspoons olive oil
- ◆ 1 (10-ounce) package sliced cremini mushrooms
- ◆ 4 scallions, thinly sliced
- 2 garlic cloves, minced
- 3/4 teaspoon salt
- ◆ 1 (6-ounce) bag baby spinach
- 2 tablespoons whole wheat bread crumbs
- ◆ 1 (2$1/2$-pound) boneless veal breast, trimmed and butterflied
- ◆ 2 large onions, cut into wedges
- 1/2 cup Madeira wine
- ◆ 1/2 cup low-sodium beef broth
- ◆ 1 tablespoon chopped fresh thyme or 1 teaspoon dried
- 1/4 cup water
- 3 tablespoons all-purpose flour

1 To make filling, heat 1 teaspoon oil in large nonstick skillet over medium-high heat. Add mushrooms, scallions, garlic, and 1/4 teaspoon salt; cook, stirring, until mushrooms are browned, 6–8 minutes. Add spinach and cook, stirring, just until spinach wilts, 1–2 minutes. Transfer vegetable mixture to bowl. Stir in bread crumbs and let cool.

2 Place veal, cut side up, on work surface. Spread filling over veal leaving 1-inch border. Starting at one narrow end, roll up jelly-roll fashion. Tie with kitchen string at 1-inch intervals. Sprinkle with remaining 1/2 teaspoon salt.

3 Heat remaining 1 teaspoon oil in skillet over medium-high heat. Add veal and cook, turning, until browned, 5 minutes. Transfer to 5-or 6-quart slow cooker. Stir in onions, wine, broth, and thyme. Cover and cook until veal is fork-tender, 3–4 hours on high or 6–8 hours on low.

4 About 35 minutes before cooking time is up, whisk water and flour in small bowl until smooth; stir in about 1/4 cup hot liquid from slow cooker until blended. Stir flour mixture into slow cooker. Cover and cook on high until mixture simmers and thickens, about 30 minutes.

5 Transfer veal to cutting board and cut crosswise in half. Transfer half of sauce (about 1$1/2$ cups) and half of veal to freezer container and let cool. Cover and freeze up to 2 months. Cut remaining veal into 8 slices. Serve with remaining 1$1/2$ cups sauce.

TO REHEAT

Thaw the veal and sauce in the refrigerator overnight. Transfer to a saucepan. Cover and cook over medium heat, turning the veal occasionally, until heated through, 15–20 minutes.

PER SERVING (2 slices with 1/3 cup sauce): 252 Cal, 8 g Fat, 3 g Sat Fat, 0 g Trans Fat, 122 mg Chol, 354 mg Sod, 11 g Carb, 2 g Fib, 32 g Prot, 78 mg Calc. *POINTS* value: 5.

White Balsamic Chicken

prep 20 min • **slow-cook** 4 hrs • **serves** 4 plus leftovers

- 1 (3$\frac{1}{2}$-pound) chicken, cut into 8 pieces and skinned
- $\frac{1}{2}$ cup dry white wine
- 3 tablespoons tomato paste with Italian seasonings
- 6 large garlic cloves, chopped
- $\frac{1}{2}$ teaspoon salt
- $\frac{1}{2}$ teaspoon coarsely ground black pepper
- 1 (14$\frac{1}{2}$-ounce) can low-sodium chicken broth
- 3 tablespoons white balsamic vinegar
- 2 tablespoons all-purpose flour
- 1 (9-ounce) package frozen sugar-snap peas, thawed
- 5 plum tomatoes, sliced $\frac{1}{2}$ inch thick

1 Place chicken in 5- or 6-quart slow cooker. Whisk wine, tomato paste, garlic, salt, and pepper in small bowl until smooth; pour over chicken. Pour 1$\frac{1}{2}$ cups broth into slow cooker. Cover and cook until chicken is fork-tender, 4–5 hours on high or 8–10 hours on low. Meanwhile, cover and refrigerate remaining broth.

2 About 30 minutes before cooking time is up, whisk reserved broth, vinegar, and flour in small bowl until smooth; stir in about $\frac{1}{4}$ cup hot liquid from slow cooker until blended. Stir flour mixture into slow cooker without disturbing chicken. Top with even layer of snap peas then tomatoes. Cover and cook on high until mixture simmers and thickens and snap peas are just tender, about 25 minutes.

3 Transfer half of sauce and vegetables (about 2 cups) and 4 pieces chicken to freezer container and let cool. Cover and freeze up to 2 months. Serve remaining 4 pieces chicken with remaining 2 cups sauce and vegetables.

TO REHEAT

Thaw the chicken and sauce in the refrigerator overnight. Transfer to a saucepan. Cover and cook over medium heat, turning the chicken occasionally, until heated through, 15–20 minutes.

PER SERVING (1 piece chicken with $\frac{1}{2}$ cup sauce and vegetables): 186 Cal, 6 g Fat, 2 g Sat Fat, 0 g Trans Fat, 65 mg Chol, 233 mg Sod, 10 g Carb, 2 g Fib, 24 g Prot, 44 mg Calc. *POINTS* value: *4.*

Thai Chicken and Squash Soup

prep 20 min • **cook/slow-cook** 3 hrs 10 min • **serves** 4 plus leftovers

- 1¼ pounds skinless, boneless chicken breasts, cut into 1-inch cubes
- ½ teaspoon salt
- 2 teaspoons canola oil
- 1 onion, chopped
- 3 garlic cloves, minced
- 1 tablespoon minced peeled fresh ginger
- 1 teaspoon Thai red curry paste
- 1 teaspoon ground cardamom
- 4 cups peeled cut-up butternut squash, cubed
- 1 (32-ounce) carton low-sodium chicken broth
- ⅔ cup light coconut milk
- 2 teaspoons packed light brown sugar
- 1 tablespoon chopped fresh chives

1 Sprinkle chicken with salt. Heat 1 teaspoon oil in large nonstick skillet over medium-high heat. Add chicken and cook, stirring occasionally, until browned, about 5 minutes. Transfer chicken to 5- or 6-quart slow cooker. Heat remaining 1 teaspoon oil in skillet over medium heat. Add onion, garlic, and ginger; cook, stirring occasionally, until onion is golden, 3–4 minutes.

2 Remove skillet from heat. Stir in curry paste and cardamom. Transfer onion mixture to slow cooker. Stir in squash and broth. Cover and cook until chicken and vegetables are fork-tender, 3–4 hours on high or 6–8 hours on low.

3 About 20 minutes before cooking time is up, stir coconut milk and brown sugar into slow cooker. Cover and cook on high until mixture simmers and flavors are blended, about 15 minutes.

4 Transfer half of soup (about 5 cups) to freezer container and let cool. Cover and freeze up to 2 months. Stir chives into remaining 5 cups soup.

TO REHEAT

Thaw the soup in the refrigerator overnight. Transfer to a saucepan. Cover and cook over medium heat, stirring occasionally, until heated through, 10–15 minutes.

PER SERVING (1¼ cups): 171 Cal, 6 g Fat, 2 g Sat Fat, 0 g Trans Fat, 44 mg Chol, 244 mg Sod, 12 g Carb, 1 g Fib, 19 g Prot, 46 mg Calc.
POINTS value: 4.

Chicken Mole

prep 25 min • **cook/slow-cook** 3 hrs 15 min • **serves** 4 plus leftovers

3   dried pasilla chile peppers, seeded

3   cups boiling water

♦ 2   cups low-sodium chicken broth

1   teaspoon olive oil

♦ 1   onion, coarsely chopped

3   garlic cloves

♦ 2   tomatoes, chopped

1/4   cup dark raisins

2   tablespoons sliced almonds, toasted

2   ounces semisweet chocolate, coarsely chopped

♦ 1   (15-ounce) can pinto beans, rinsed and drained

♦ 8   (1/4-pound) skinless chicken thighs

1/2   teaspoon salt

1 Heat large nonstick skillet over medium-high heat. Open chiles flat. Place them in skillet in single layer and press down firmly with spatula. Toast until crackly and just beginning to smoke, about 30 seconds per side. Transfer to bowl. Add boiling water and let stand until softened, about 20 minutes. Drain and discard liquid. Puree chiles and 1 cup broth in food processor. Transfer puree to 5- or 6-quart slow cooker.

2 Heat oil in skillet over medium-high heat. Add onion and garlic; cook, stirring occasionally, until onion is golden, 3–4 minutes. Add tomatoes and cook, stirring occasionally, until softened, about 2 minutes. Transfer tomato mixture to food processor. Add remaining 1 cup broth, raisins, almonds, and chocolate and puree. Transfer mixture to slow cooker and stir in beans.

3 Wipe skillet clean. Sprinkle chicken with salt. Spray skillet with nonstick spray and set over medium-high heat. Add chicken and cook until browned, about 4 minutes per side. Transfer chicken to slow cooker. Press chicken down into chile mixture. Cover and cook until chicken is fork-tender, 3–4 hours on high or 6–8 hours on low.

4 With slotted spoon, transfer 4 thighs to freezer container. Top with half of sauce (about 2 1/2 cups) and let cool. Cover and freeze up to 2 months. Divide remaining 4 thighs and 2 1/2 cups sauce among 4 plates.

TO REHEAT

Thaw the chicken and sauce in the refrigerator overnight. Transfer to a saucepan. Cover and cook over medium heat, stirring occasionally, until heated through, about 15 minutes.

PER SERVING (1 chicken thigh with generous 1/2 cup sauce): 255 Cal, 10 g Fat, 3 g Sat Fat, 0 g Trans Fat, 43 mg Chol, 263 mg Sod, 23 g Carb, 5 g Fib, 20 g Prot, 54 mg Calc. *POINTS* value: *5.*

Brandy Chicken with Dried Plums and Olives

prep 15 min • cook/slow-cook 3 hrs 20 min • serves 4 plus leftovers

2   teaspoons olive oil

♦ 4   (5-ounce) skinless chicken thighs

♦ 4   (^{1}/4-pound) skinless chicken drumsticks

♦ 1   large onion, thinly sliced

♦ 1   (14^1/2-ounce) can stewed tomatoes

♦ ^{3}/4   cup low-sodium chicken broth

^{1}/3   cup brandy

12   pitted dried plums

♦ 12   brine-cured green olives, pitted

3   garlic cloves, finely chopped

1 Heat 1 teaspoon oil in large nonstick skillet over medium-high heat. Add thighs and cook until browned, about 3 minutes per side. Transfer to 5 or 6-quart slow cooker. Repeat with remaining 1 teaspoon oil and drumsticks.

2 Add onion to skillet. Reduce heat and cook, stirring occasionally, until softened, 6–8 minutes. Stir in tomatoes, broth, brandy, plums, olives, and garlic; cook, scraping browned bits from bottom of pan, until mixture comes to a boil. Pour tomato mixture over chicken. Cover and cook until chicken and onion are fork-tender, 3–4 hours on high or 6–8 hours on low.

3 Transfer 2 thighs, 2 drumsticks, and half of sauce (about 2 cups) to freezer container and let cool. Cover and freeze up to 2 months. Divide remaining 2 thighs, 2 drumsticks, and 2 cups sauce among 4 plates.

TO REHEAT

Thaw the chicken and sauce in the refrigerator overnight. Transfer to a saucepan. Cover and cook over medium heat, stirring occasionally, until heated through, about 15 minutes.

PER SERVING (1 piece chicken with ^{1}/2 cup sauce): 190 Cal, 7 g Fat, 2 g Sat Fat, 0 g Trans Fat, 53 mg Chol, 203 mg Sod, 14 g Carb, 2 g Fib, 17 g Prot, 48 mg Calc. *POINTS* value: *4.*

Rosemary Chicken with Bell Peppers

prep 15 min • cook/slow-cook 3 hrs 10 min • serves 4 plus leftovers

2 teaspoons canola oil

♦ 3 assorted-color bell peppers, sliced

♦ 1 onion, sliced

3/4 teaspoon salt

♦ 1 (14 1/2-ounce) can stewed tomatoes

♦ 1 cup low-sodium chicken broth

1 tablespoon chopped fresh rosemary or 1 teaspoon dried

1 tablespoon fennel seeds, crushed

♦ 8 skinless chicken drumsticks

♦ 1 cup whole wheat orzo

1 Heat 1 teaspoon oil in large nonstick skillet over medium-high heat. Add bell peppers, onion, and 1/4 teaspoon salt; cook, stirring occasionally, until softened, 6–8 minutes. Transfer bell pepper mixture to 5- or 6-quart slow cooker. Stir in tomatoes and broth.

2 Combine rosemary, fennel, and remaining 1/2 teaspoon salt in large bowl. Add chicken; toss to coat. Heat remaining 1 teaspoon oil in skillet over medium-high heat. Add chicken and cook, turning occasionally, until browned, 4–5 minutes. Transfer chicken to slow cooker. Press chicken down into bell pepper mixture. Cover and cook until chicken and vegetables are fork-tender, 3–4 hours on high or 6–8 hours on low.

3 About 20 minutes before cooking time is up, cook orzo according to package directions, omitting salt if desired.

4 Transfer 4 drumsticks with slotted spoon to freezer container. Top with half of sauce (about 2 cups) and let cool. Cover and freeze up to 2 months. Divide remaining 4 drumsticks and 2 cups sauce among 4 plates. Serve with orzo.

TO REHEAT

Thaw the chicken and sauce in the refrigerator overnight. Transfer to a saucepan. Cover and cook over medium heat, stirring occasionally, until heated through, 10–12 minutes. This recipe works with the Simply Filling technique.

PER SERVING (1 drumstick with 1/2 cup sauce and 3/4 cup orzo): 252 Cal, 4 g Fat, 1 g Sat Fat, 0 g Trans Fat, 49 mg Chol, 549 mg Sod, 36 g Carb, 5 g Fib, 20 g Prot, 59 mg Calc. *POINTS* value: *5.*

Mexi-Style Meatball Soup

prep 25 min • cook/slow-cook 3 hrs 5 min • serves 4 plus leftovers

1 (20-ounce) package hot or sweet Italian turkey sausage links, casings removed

♦ 1/4 cup cornmeal

♦ 1 large egg, lightly beaten

1/2 teaspoon ground cumin

1/4 teaspoon ground allspice

♦ 1 onion, finely chopped

♦ 1 carrot, diced

2 garlic cloves, minced

♦ 1 (32-ounce) carton low-sodium chicken broth

♦ 1 (14 1/2-ounce) can diced tomatoes with jalapeños

♦ 1 (5-ounce) package baby spinach

♦ 2 tablespoons chopped scallions

1 Combine sausage, cornmeal, egg, cumin, and allspice in medium bowl. With moistened hands, form into 30 meatballs. Transfer meatballs to 5- or 6-quart slow cooker.

2 Spray medium nonstick skillet with nonstick spray and set over medium-high heat. Add onion, carrot, and garlic; cook, stirring occasionally, until vegetables are softened, about 5 minutes. Transfer vegetables to slow cooker; stir in broth and tomatoes. Cover and cook until vegetables are fork-tender and instant-read thermometer inserted into center of meatball registers 180°F, 3–4 hours on high or 6–8 hours on low.

3 About 10 minutes before cooking time is up, stir spinach into slow cooker. Cover and cook on high just until spinach begins to wilt, about 5 minutes.

4 Transfer half of soup (about 4 cups) to freezer container and let cool. Cover and freeze up to 2 months. Ladle remaining soup evenly among 4 bowls. Serve, sprinkled with scallions.

TO REHEAT
Thaw the soup in the refrigerator overnight. Transfer to a saucepan. Cover and cook over medium heat, stirring occasionally, until heated through, 10–12 minutes.

PER SERVING (1 cup): 209 Cal, 9 g Fat, 2 g Sat Fat, 0 g Trans Fat, 92 mg Chol, 604 mg Sod, 11 g Carb, 2 g Fib, 22 g Prot, 71 mg Calc.
POINTS value: 5.

Cod Vera Cruz

prep 25 min • cook/slow-cook 1 hr 10 min • serves 4 plus leftovers

2   teaspoons olive oil

♦ 1   onion, sliced

3   garlic cloves, finely chopped

♦ 2   (14 1/2-ounce) can petite diced tomatoes

1/2   cup dry white wine or clam juice

♦ 1/4   cup small pimiento-stuffed green olives (about 20)

3   tablespoons raisins

2   tablespoons capers

1   teaspoon dried oregano

1/2   teaspoon salt

1/4   teaspoon red pepper flakes

♦ 8   (6-ounce) skinless cod fillets

Grated zest of 1/2 lemon

1 Heat oil in large nonstick skillet over medium-high heat. Add onion and garlic; cook, stirring occasionally, until onion is softened, about 5 minutes. Stir in tomatoes, wine, olives, raisins, capers, oregano, salt, and red pepper flakes; bring to boil. Transfer tomato mixture to 5- or 6-quart slow cooker. Add cod fillets to slow cooker. Gently press fillets down into tomato mixture. Cover and cook until onion is fork-tender and each fillet is just opaque in center, 1–2 hours on high or 2–4 hours on low.

2 Transfer 4 fillets with slotted spoon to freezer container. Top with half of sauce (about 2 1/4 cups) and let cool. Cover and freeze up to 1 month. Divide remaining 4 fillets and 2 1/4 cups sauce among 4 plates. Serve, sprinkled with lemon zest.

TO REHEAT

Thaw the fillets and sauce in the refrigerator overnight. Transfer to a skillet. Cover and cook over medium heat until heated through, 10–15 minutes, turning the fillets once halfway through the cooking time.

PER SERVING (1 fillet with generous 1/2 cup sauce): 211 Cal, 4 g Fat, 1 g Sat Fat, 0 g Trans Fat, 90 mg Chol, 571 mg Sod, 9 g Carb, 2 g Fib, 33 g Prot, 70 mg Calc. *POINTS* value: *4.*

Monkfish Ragú

prep 25 min • slow-cook 2 hrs 40 min • serves 4 plus leftovers

- ◆ 1 (28-ounce) can diced tomatoes, drained (no salt added)
- ◆ 1 cup low-sodium chicken broth
- 1/2 **cup clam juice**
- ◆ 1 large red onion, chopped
- ◆ 1/2 fennel bulb, chopped
- ◆ 1 Cubanelle pepper, seeded and chopped
- 2 **garlic cloves, minced**
- ◆ 1/4 cup tomato paste (no salt added)
- 2 **tablespoons sherry vinegar**
- 1 **tablespoon chopped fresh thyme or 1 teaspoon dried**
- 1 **teaspoon fennel seeds**
- 1/2 **teaspoon red pepper flakes**
- 1/2 **teaspoon salt**
- ◆ 2 pounds monkfish, cut into 1-inch chunks
- ◆ 1 pound Swiss chard, stems removed and leaves coarsely chopped

1 Combine tomatoes, broth, clam juice, onion, fennel, Cubanelle pepper, garlic, tomato paste, vinegar, thyme, fennel seeds, red pepper flakes, and salt in 5- or 6-quart slow cooker. Cover and cook until mixture simmers and tomatoes have softened, 2–3 hours on high.

2 At end of cooking time, gently stir in monkfish and Swiss chard. Cover and cook on high until monkfish is just opaque in center, about 40 minutes.

3 Transfer half of ragú (about 5 cups) to freezer container and let cool. Cover and freeze up to 1 month. Divide remaining 5 cups ragú among 4 plates.

TO REHEAT

Thaw the ragú in the refrigerator overnight. Transfer to a saucepan. Cover and cook over medium heat until heated through, 10–15 minutes, stirring once halfway through the cooking time. This recipe works with the Simply Filling technique.

PER SERVING (1 1/4 cups): 184 Cal, 5 g Fat, 1 g Sat Fat, 0 g Trans Fat, 42 mg Chol, 511 mg Sod, 13 g Carb, 4 g Fib, 24 g Prot, 73 mg Calc.
POINTS value: *3.*

Shrimp Creole

prep 20 min • **cook/slow cook** 3 hrs 10 min • **serves** 4 plus leftovers

2	teaspoons olive oil
♦ 4	celery stalks, sliced
♦ 2	assorted-color bell peppers, sliced
♦ 1	onion, sliced
♦ 4	plum tomatoes, chopped
3	garlic cloves, chopped
$^1/_2$	teaspoon Creole seasoning
♦ $1^1/_2$	cups low-sodium chicken broth
3	tablespoons water
2	tablespoons all-purpose flour
♦ 2	pounds large shrimp, shelled and deveined
♦ 1	(10-ounce) box frozen peas, thawed
♦ 3	cups hot cooked brown rice

1 Heat oil in large nonstick skillet over medium-high heat. Add celery, bell peppers, and onion; cook, stirring occasionally, until vegetables are softened, 6–8 minutes. Add tomatoes, garlic, and Creole seasoning; cook, stirring occasionally, until tomatoes have softened, 5–6 minutes. Transfer mixture to 5- or 6-quart slow cooker. Stir in broth. Cover and cook until vegetables are fork-tender, 3–4 hours on high or 6–8 hours on low.

2 About 30 minutes before cooking time is up, whisk water and flour in small bowl until smooth; stir in about $^1/_4$ cup hot liquid from slow cooker until blended. Stir flour mixture, shrimp, and peas into slow cooker. Cover and cook on high until mixture simmers and thickens and shrimp are just opaque in center, about 25 minutes.

3 Transfer half of shrimp mixture (about 4 cups) to freezer container and let cool. Cover and freeze up to 1 month. Serve remaining 4 cups shrimp mixture with rice.

TO REHEAT

Thaw the shrimp mixture in the refrigerator overnight. Transfer to a saucepan. Cover and cook over medium heat, stirring occasionally, until heated through, 12–15 minutes.

PER SERVING ($1^1/_4$ cups shrimp mixture with $^3/_4$ cup rice): 293 Cal, 4 g Fat, 1 g Sat Fat, 0 g Trans Fat, 107 mg Chol, 219 mg Sod, 46 g Carb, 8 g Fib, 19 g Prot, 66 mg Calc. *POINTS* value: *5.*

Root Vegetable Tagine

prep 25 min • **cook/slow-cook** 3 hr 5 min • **serves** 4 plus leftovers

2   teaspoons canola oil

♦ 1   onion, sliced

2   garlic cloves, chopped

1   teaspoon cinnamon

1/2   teaspoon ground cumin

1/2   teaspoon ground ginger

♦ 2   sweet potatoes, peeled and cut into 1-inch chunks

♦ 2   carrots, sliced 1/2 inch thick

♦ 2   small tomatoes, chopped

♦ 1   parsnip, peeled and cut into 1-inch chunks

1/2   cup pitted dried plums

♦ 3   cups vegetable broth

1   tablespoon honey

♦ 3/4   cup whole wheat couscous

1/4   cup sliced almonds, toasted

1 Heat oil in medium nonstick skillet over medium-high heat. Add onion and garlic; cook, stirring occasionally, until onion is softened, 5–6 minutes. Remove skillet from heat; stir in cinnamon, cumin, and ginger. Transfer onion mixture to 5- or 6-quart slow cooker. Add potatoes, carrots, tomatoes, parsnip, and dried plums. Combine broth and honey in large bowl; stir into vegetable mixture. Cover and cook until vegetables are fork-tender, 3–4 hours on low or 6–8 hours on high.

2 About 15 minutes before cooking time is up, cook couscous according to package directions, omitting salt if desired.

3 Transfer half of tagine (about 4 1/2 cups) to freezer container and let cool. Cover and freeze up to 2 months. Divide remaining 4 1/2 cups tagine among 4 plates. Sprinkle with almonds and serve with couscous.

TO REHEAT
Thaw the tagine in the refrigerator overnight. Transfer to a saucepan. Cover and cook over medium heat, stirring occasionally, until heated through, 12–15 minutes.

PER SERVING (generous 1 cup tagine with 1 tablespoon almonds and 1/2 cup couscous): 231 Cal, 4 g Fat, 0 g Sat Fat, 0 g Trans Fat, 0 mg Chol, 378 mg Sod, 47 g Carb, 8 g Fib, 6 g Prot, 68 mg Calc. *POINTS* value: *4.*

CATALAN SEAFOOD STE
PAGE 150

Chapter 5

Beans and Grains

Hearty main dishes, soups, sides, (even breads!) the whole family will love.

Barley, Beef, and Root Vegetable Stew

prep 25 min • **cook/slow-cook** 3 hrs 10 min • **serves** 4

- ½ pound bottom round steak, trimmed and cut into ½-inch cubes
- 1 onion, chopped
- 1 cup water
- 4 carrots, quartered lengthwise and cut into ½-inch chunks
- 1 celeriac, peeled and cut into ¾-inch chunks
- 2 parsnips, peeled and cut into ¾-inch chunks
- 1 turnip, peeled and cut into ¾-inch chunks
- 1 (14½-ounce) can low-sodium beef broth
- ½ cup pearl barley
- 3 garlic cloves, minced
- 1 tablespoon chopped fresh thyme or 1 teaspoon dried
- ½ teaspoon salt
- ¼ teaspoon black pepper

1 Spray large nonstick skillet with nonstick spray and set over medium-high heat. Add beef and cook, stirring frequently, until browned, about 4 minutes. Transfer beef to 5- or 6-quart slow cooker.

2 Add onion to skillet and cook, stirring frequently, until lightly browned, about 4 minutes. Add water and cook, scraping up browned bits from bottom of pan. Pour onion mixture into slow cooker. Stir in carrots, celeriac, parsnips, turnip, broth, barley, garlic, thyme, salt, and pepper. Cover and cook until beef and vegetables are fork-tender, 3–4 hours on high or 6–8 hours on low.

♦ FILLING EXTRA

For even heartier flavor, add a 10-ounce package sliced cremini or white mushrooms with the vegetables in step 2. This recipe works with the Simply Filling technique.

PER SERVING (1½ cups): 306 Cal, 4 g Fat, 1 g Sat Fat, 0 g Trans Fat, 42 mg Chol, 477 mg Sod, 46 g Carb, 10 g Fib, 24 g Prot, 100 mg Calc.
POINTS value: *6.*

Pinto, Pork, and Hominy Stew

prep 20 min • **cook/slow-cook** 3 hrs 5 min • **serves** 4

- ◆ $1/2$ pound boneless pork loin, trimmed and cut into $1/2$-inch cubes
- ◆ 1 onion, chopped
- $1/2$ cup water
- ◆ 1 ($15^{1}/_{2}$-ounce) can pinto beans, rinsed and drained
- ◆ 1 ($14^{1}/_{2}$-ounce) can low-sodium chicken broth
- ◆ 1 large red bell pepper, thinly sliced
- ◆ 1 cup fresh or thawed frozen corn kernels
- 2 garlic cloves, minced
- 1 ($1^{1}/_{4}$-ounce) envelope low-sodium chili seasoning mix
- 1 teaspoon ground cumin
- ◆ 1 (15-ounce) can hominy, rinsed and drained
- ◆ 4 radishes, chopped
- 2 tablespoons chopped fresh cilantro

1 Spray large nonstick skillet with nonstick spray and set over medium-high heat. Add pork and onion; cook, stirring frequently, until browned, about 5 minutes. Transfer pork mixture to 5- or 6-quart slow cooker.

2 Add water to skillet and cook, scraping up browned bits from bottom of pan. Pour liquid into slow cooker; stir in beans, broth, bell pepper, corn, garlic, seasoning mix, and cumin. Top with hominy. Cover and cook until pork and vegetables are fork-tender, 3–4 hours on high or 6–8 hours on low. Serve, sprinkled with radishes and cilantro.

IN THE KITCHEN

Hominy are dried corn kernels with a pleasantly chewy texture and mild flavor. Look for the canned variety near the canned beans at the supermarket.

PER SERVING ($1^{1}/_{4}$ cups): 362 Cal, 7 g Fat, 2 g Sat Fat, 0 g Trans Fat, 36 mg Chol, 520 mg Sod, 51 g Carb, 13 g Fib, 25 g Prot, 95 mg Calc. *POINTS* value: *7.*

Pasta e Fagioli Soup

prep 20 min • cook/slow-cook 4 hrs 5 min • serves 6

2   teaspoons extra-virgin olive oil

♦ 1   large red onion, finely chopped

3   garlic cloves, finely chopped

1   tablespoon chopped fresh rosemary or 1 teaspoon dried

♦ 1   (19-ounce) can cannellini (white kidney) beans, rinsed and drained

♦ 3   carrots, finely chopped

♦ 1   fennel bulb, finely chopped

1   (3-ounce) piece smoked ham hock

12   fresh flat-leaf parsley sprigs

1/2   teaspoon salt

1/4   teaspoon black pepper

♦ 1   (32-ounce) carton low-sodium chicken broth

1   cup ditalini

1/4   cup grated pecorino cheese

1 Heat oil in large nonstick skillet over medium heat. Add onion, garlic, and rosemary; cook, stirring occasionally, until onion is softened, about 5 minutes. Transfer onion mixture to 5- or 6-quart slow cooker. Stir in beans, carrots, fennel, ham hock, parsley, salt, and pepper. Pour broth over beans and vegetables. Cover and cook until vegetables are fork-tender, 4–5 hours on high or 8–10 hours on low. Discard ham hock and parsley. Skim any fat from soup.

2 About 20 minutes before cooking time is up, cook ditalini according to package directions, omitting salt if desired.

3 At end of cooking time, stir ditalini into slow cooker. Serve, sprinkled with pecorino.

♦ FILLING EXTRA

If you like, before sprinkling the soup with the pecorino in step 3, top it evenly with 3 seeded and finely diced plum tomatoes.

PER SERVING (2 cups): 247 Cal, 7 g Fat, 2 g Sat Fat, 0 g Trans Fat, 18 mg Chol, 1,027 mg Sod, 30 g Carb, 6 g Fib, 17 g Prot, 101 mg Calc. *POINTS* value: *5.*

Escarole, Bean, and Chicken Soup

prep 20 min • **slow-cook** 3 hrs 25 min • **serves** 6

- ♦ 2 (10-ounce) bone-in chicken breasts, skinned
- ♦ 4 carrots, sliced
- ♦ 2 celery stalks, sliced
- ♦ 1 onion, finely chopped
- **2 garlic cloves, minced**
- ♦ 5 cups low-sodium chicken broth
- $1/2$ **teaspoon Italian seasoning**
- $1/2$ **teaspoon salt**
- $1/4$ **teaspoon black pepper**
- ♦ 1 small head escarole, trimmed and cut into 1-inch pieces
- ♦ 1 (15-ounce) can white beans, rinsed and drained
- **3 ounces multigrain spaghetti, broken into $1^1/2$-inch lengths**
- $1/4$ **cup grated Parmesan cheese**

1 Place chicken in 5- or 6-quart slow cooker. Top with carrots, celery, onion, and garlic. Add broth, Italian seasoning, salt, and pepper. Cover and cook until chicken and vegetables are fork-tender, 3–4 hours on high or 6–8 hours on low.

2 At end of cooking time, transfer chicken with slotted spoon to plate and let stand until cool enough to handle, about 20 minutes.

3 Meanwhile, stir escarole, beans, and spaghetti into slow cooker. Cover and cook on high until escarole and spaghetti are tender, about 20 minutes, stirring once halfway through cooking time.

4 Remove chicken from bones and coarsely shred. Stir chicken into slow cooker. Cover and cook on high until heated through, about 5 minutes. Serve, sprinkled with Parmesan.

IN THE KITCHEN

If the soup seems thick after cooking the escarole and spaghetti, add an additional 1 cup low-sodium chicken broth with the shredded chicken in step 4.

PER SERVING (about $1^2/3$ cups soup with 2 teaspoons cheese): 326 Cal, 6 g Fat, 2 g Sat Fat, 0 g Trans Fat, 62 mg Chol, 579 mg Sod, 34 g Carb, 6 g Fib, 35 g Prot, 161 mg Calc. *POINTS* value: 6.

Brown and Wild Rice Casserole with Chicken

prep 15 min • cook/slow-cook 2 hrs 35 min • serves 6

- ◆ 1 small onion, chopped
- ◆ 2$\frac{1}{2}$ cups low-sodium chicken broth
- ◆ 6 small carrots, cut diagonally into $\frac{1}{2}$-inch slices
- ◆ 1 (8-ounce) package sliced mushrooms
- ◆ 1 cup brown and wild rice blend or $\frac{1}{2}$ cup each brown rice and wild rice
- ◆ 2 celery stalks, cut diagonally into $\frac{1}{2}$-inch slices
- 2 garlic cloves, minced
- $\frac{1}{2}$ teaspoon poultry seasoning
- $\frac{1}{4}$ teaspoon salt
- ◆ 1$\frac{1}{4}$ pounds chicken tenders
- 1 (10$\frac{3}{4}$-ounce) can low-fat condensed cream of mushroom soup

1 Spray large nonstick skillet with nonstick spray and set over medium heat. Add onion and cook, stirring occasionally, until softened, about 5 minutes. Transfer onion to 5- or 6-quart slow cooker. Stir in broth, carrots, mushrooms, rice blend, celery, garlic, poultry seasoning, and salt; mix well. Top with chicken, placing it towards center of slow cooker. Cover and cook until chicken and vegetables are fork-tender and rice is tender but still slightly chewy, 2$\frac{1}{2}$–3 hours on high or 5–6 hours on low.

2 About 25 minutes before cooking time is up, stir soup into slow cooker. Cover and cook on high until mixture simmers, about 20 minutes.

◆ FILLING EXTRA
Prepare the recipe as directed, but add 3 cups thawed frozen peas to the slow cooker with the soup in step 2 and up the per-serving **POINTS** value by **1.**

PER SERVING (1$\frac{1}{3}$ cups): 309 Cal, 6 g Fat, 2 g Sat Fat, 0 g Trans Fat, 60 mg Chol, 625 mg Sod, 35 g Carb, 5 g Fib, 29 g Prot, 63 mg Calc.
POINTS value: *6.*

Cornmeal Dumplings with Beans, Greens, and Chicken

prep 25 min • **slow-cook** 3 hrs 25 min • **serves** 6

- 1 onion, finely chopped
- **2 garlic cloves, minced**
- **1/4 teaspoon salt**
- 3/4 pound skinless, boneless chicken thighs, halved
- 1 (15-ounce) can white beans, rinsed and drained
- 1 pound collard greens, stems discarded, leaves cut into 1-inch pieces
- 1/2 pound kale, stems discarded, leaves cut into 1-inch pieces
- 2 (14-ounce) cans low-sodium chicken broth
- **3/4 cup low-fat buttermilk baking mix**
- 1/4 cup cornmeal
- 1/3 cup fat-free milk
- **White vinegar and hot pepper sauce (optional)**

1 Combine onion, garlic, and salt in 5- or 6-quart slow cooker. In single layers, top with chicken, beans, collard greens, and kale. Press greens down into slow cooker to fit. Pour broth over greens. Cover and cook until chicken and greens are fork-tender, 3–4 hours on high or 6–8 hours on low.

2 At end of cooking time, transfer greens with slotted spoon to bowl; cover and keep warm.

3 Combine baking mix and cornmeal in medium bowl. Stir in milk just until soft dough forms. Drop dough by heaping tablespoonfuls about 1 inch apart onto simmering stew, making 6 dumplings. Cover and cook on high until toothpick inserted in center of each dumpling comes out clean, 25–30 minutes.

4 Divide greens among 6 shallow bowls. Top evenly with chicken and beans mixture and dumplings. Serve with vinegar and pepper sauce (if using).

PER SERVING (2/3 cup greens with about 2/3 cup chicken and bean mixture and 1 dumpling): 298 Cal, 7 g Fat, 2 g Sat Fat, 0 g Trans Fat, 35 mg Chol, 507 mg Sod, 37 g Carb, 7 g Fib, 24 g Prot, 253 mg Calc. *POINTS* value: **6.**

Golden Split Pea Soup

prep 20 min • **slow-cook/cook** 4 hrs 5 min • **serves** 6

- 1 (48-ounce) can low-sodium chicken broth
- **2 cups water**
- 1 cup dried yellow split peas, picked over, rinsed, and drained
- 1 cup dried red lentils, picked over, rinsed, and drained
- 2 carrots, diced
- 2 celery stalks, diced
- 1 onion, chopped
- 1 sweet potato, peeled and diced
- **2 garlic cloves, minced**
- **1 tablespoon curry powder**
- **1/2 teaspoon salt**
- 1 (10-ounce) smoked turkey drumstick

1 Combine broth, water, split peas, lentils, carrots, celery, onion, potato, garlic, curry powder, and salt in 5- or 6-quart slow cooker. Add turkey, pressing it down into broth mixture. Cover and cook until peas, lentils, and vegetables are fork-tender, 4–5 hours on high or 8–10 hours on low.

2 At end of cooking time, transfer turkey with slotted spoon to plate and let stand until cool enough to handle, about 15 minutes.

3 Remove and discard skin and bones from turkey; cut turkey into bite-size chunks. Stir turkey into slow cooker. Cover and cook on high until hot, about 5 minutes.

♦ FILLING EXTRA

Top each serving of this chunky soup with **1 tablespoon** plain fat-free yogurt. This recipe works with the Simply Filling technique.

PER SERVING (1 1/2 cups): 312 Cal, 3 g Fat, 1 g Sat Fat, 0 g Trans Fat, 25 mg Chol, 655 mg Sod, 47 g Carb, 16 g Fib, 27 g Prot, 75 mg Calc. *POINTS* value: **6.**

Turkey-and-Bean Burrito Bake

prep 30 min • cook/slow-cook 2 hrs 35 min • serves 6

- ◆ $3/4$ pound ground skinless turkey breast
- ◆ 1 onion, finely chopped
-   1 tablespoon chili powder
- ◆ 1 ($14^1/2$-ounce) can diced tomatoes
-   1 (10-ounce) can enchilada sauce
- ◆ 1 cup fat-free salsa
-   6 fat-free corn tortillas
- ◆ $1/2$ cup quick-cooking brown rice
- ◆ 1 zucchini, chopped
- ◆ 1 (15-ounce) can pink or red beans, rinsed and drained
-   $1^1/3$ cups shredded low-fat Mexican cheese blend
- ◆ 3 cups shredded lettuce
- ◆ $1/3$ cup fat-free sour cream

1 Spray large nonstick skillet with nonstick spray and set over medium-high heat. Add turkey and onion; cook, breaking turkey apart with wooden spoon, until turkey is no longer pink, about 5 minutes. Stir in chili powder and remove skillet from heat.

2 Spray 5- or 6-quart slow cooker stoneware with nonstick spray. Combine tomatoes, enchilada sauce, and $1/3$ cup salsa in medium bowl. Spread $1/2$ cup tomato mixture over bottom of slow cooker. Top with 2 tortillas, tearing one of the tortillas in half so tortillas cover tomato mixture. Top evenly with half of turkey mixture, half of rice, and half of zucchini. Spoon 1 cup tomato mixture evenly over zucchini. Top with half of beans and $1/2$ cup cheese blend. Repeat with 2 tortillas, remaining turkey mixture, rice, and zucchini, 1 cup tomato mixture, remaining beans, and $1/2$ cup cheese blend. Top with remaining 2 tortillas and spread with remaining tomato mixture. Cover and cook until hot and bubbling at edges, $2^1/2$–3 hours on high or 5–6 hours on low.

3 Sprinkle burrito bake with remaining $1/3$ cup cheese blend. Cover and let stand until cheese melts, about 5 minutes. Serve with remaining $2/3$ cup salsa, the lettuce and sour cream.

PER SERVING ($1^1/2$ cups burrito bake with $1^1/2$ tablespoons salsa, $1/2$ cup lettuce, and 1 tablespoon sour cream): 341 Cal, 7 g Fat, 3 g Sat Fat, 0 g Trans Fat, 53 mg Chol, 956 mg Sod, 45 g Carb, 10 g Fib, 28 g Prot, 380 mg Calc. *POINTS* value: 7.

Polenta Lasagna

prep 30 min • cook/slow-cook 2 hrs 45 min • serves 6

3/4 **pound hot Italian turkey sausage links, casings removed**

♦ 1 (8-ounce) package sliced mushrooms

1 **(24-ounce) jar fat-free marinara sauce**

♦ 1 (18-ounce) tube refrigerated fat-free plain polenta, cut into 18 rounds

♦ 1 (10-ounce) package frozen chopped spinach, thawed and squeezed dry

♦ 1 cup fat-free ricotta cheese

♦ 1 zucchini, very thinly sliced

♦ 3/4 cup shredded fat-free mozzarella cheese

1/4 **cup grated Parmesan cheese**

1 Place large nonstick skillet over medium heat. Add sausage and cook, breaking it apart with wooden spoon, until no longer pink, about 8 minutes. Transfer sausage with slotted spoon to plate. Add mushrooms to skillet and cook, stirring occasionally, until liquid is absorbed and mushrooms are tender, about 5 minutes.

2 Spray 5- or 6-quart slow cooker stoneware with nonstick spray. Spread 1/3 cup marinara sauce in bottom of slow cooker. Top with 6 slices polenta (if they don't cover bottom completely that's okay), half of spinach, and half of mushrooms. Spread 1/2 cup ricotta over mushrooms and spinach. Top with half of sausage, 1 cup marinara sauce, and half of zucchini. Repeat with 6 slices polenta, remaining spinach, mushrooms, ricotta, and sausage, 1 cup marinara sauce, and remaining zucchini. Top with remaining 6 polenta slices and marinara sauce. Cover and cook until lasagna is hot and bubbling, 2 1/2–3 hours on high or 5–6 hours on low.

3 Turn off slow cooker. Sprinkle lasagna with mozzarella and Parmesan. Cover and let stand 20 minutes before serving. Cut into 6 wedges.

PER SERVING (1 wedge): 297 Cal, 8 g Fat, 2 g Sat Fat, 0 g Trans Fat, 62 mg Chol, 1,147 mg Sod, 27 g Carb, 4 g Fib, 30 g Prot, 350 mg Calc. *POINTS* value: *6.*

Salmon Risotto

prep 15 min • cook/slow-cook 2 hrs 15 min • serves 6

♦ 1 onion, chopped

♦ 1 1/2 cups red and brown rice blend or brown rice

2 garlic cloves, crushed through a press

1/2 cup dry white wine or clam juice

♦ 1 (32-ounce) carton low-sodium chicken broth

♦ 1 1/2 cups shredded carrots

3/4 teaspoon salt

1/4 teaspoon black pepper

♦ 1 pound skinless salmon fillet, cut into 1-inch chunks

♦ 1 cup frozen peas, thawed

1 Spray large nonstick skillet with nonstick spray and set over medium heat. Add onion and cook, stirring frequently, until softened, about 5 minutes. Add rice blend and garlic; cook, stirring frequently, until rice is translucent, about 2 minutes. Add wine and cook, stirring frequently, until wine is absorbed, about 1 minute.

2 Transfer rice mixture to 5- or 6-quart slow cooker. Stir in broth, carrots, salt, and pepper. Cover and cook until rice is tender, but still slightly chewy, 2–2 1/2 hours on high or 4–5 hours on low.

3 About 15 minutes before cooking time is up, stir salmon and peas into slow cooker. Cover and cook on high until salmon is just opaque in center and peas are just tender, 15–20 minutes, stirring once halfway through cooking time.

♦ FILLING EXTRA

For an extra-fancy seafood risotto, prepare the recipe as directed but add 3/4 pound shelled and deveined cooked shrimp along with the salmon in step 3 (and up the per-serving *POINTS* value by *1*).

PER SERVING (1 1/3 cups): 345 Cal, 7 g Fat, 2 g Sat Fat, 0 g Trans Fat, 50 mg Chol, 429 mg Sod, 46 g Carb, 7 g Fib, 25 g Prot, 53 mg Calc. *POINTS* value: *7*.

Catalan Seafood Stew

prep 25 min • cook/slow-cook 3 hrs 15 min • serves 6

♦ 1   onion, sliced

  2   garlic cloves, crushed through a press

1½ teaspoons ground cumin

1½ teaspoons smoked paprika

¼   teaspoon salt

⅛   to ¼ teaspoon red pepper flakes

♦ 1   (15-ounce) can kidney beans, rinsed and drained

♦ 1   (15-ounce) can chickpeas, rinsed and drained

♦ 1   (14½-ounce) can fire-roasted diced tomatoes

♦ 1   cup low-sodium chicken broth

♦ 1   bell pepper (any color), cut into 1-inch chunks

♦ ⅔   cup farro or brown rice

♦ ½   pound skinless halibut or cod fillet, cut into 1-inch chunks

♦ ½   pound large shrimp, peeled and deveined

  ½   cup fresh cilantro leaves

1 Spray large nonstick skillet with nonstick spray and set over medium heat. Add onion and cook until softened, about 5 minutes. Stir in garlic, cumin, paprika, salt, and red pepper flakes. Transfer onion mixture to 5- or 6-quart slow cooker. Stir in beans, chickpeas, tomatoes, bell pepper, and broth. Cover and cook until vegetables are fork-tender, 3–4 hours on high or 6–8 hours on low.

2 About 40 minutes before cooking time is up, cook farro according to package directions.

3 At end of cooking time, stir halibut and shrimp into slow cooker. Cover and cook on high until halibut and shrimp are just opaque in center, 8–10 minutes.

4 Divide farro evenly among 4 plates; top evenly with stew. Serve, sprinkled with cilantro.

IN THE KITCHEN

Farro are whole wheat kernels from Italy prized for their sweet and nutty flavor. Look for semi-pearled farro, which requires no presoaking. This recipe works with the Simply Filling technique.

PER SERVING (generous 1 cup stew with about ⅓ cup farro): 297 Cal, 3 g Fat, 1 g Sat Fat, 0 g Trans Fat, 56 mg Chol, 470 mg Sod, 46 g Carb, 10 g Fib, 24 g Prot, 101 mg Calc. *POINTS* value: *5.*

Shrimp and Lentil Curry

prep 20 min • **slow-cook** 2 hrs 15 min • **serves** 4

- 2¹/₂ cups low-sodium vegetable broth
- 1 cup dried red lentils, picked over, rinsed, and drained
- 1 large red onion, chopped
- 2 celery stalks, thinly sliced
- 2 tablespoons minced peeled fresh ginger
- 1 garlic clove, minced
- 4 teaspoons curry powder
- ¹/₂ teaspoon cinnamon
- ¹/₂ teaspoon salt
- ¹/₈ teaspoon cayenne
- 2 pounds medium shrimp, peeled and deveined

1 Combine broth, lentils, onion, celery, ginger, garlic, curry powder, cinnamon, salt, and cayenne in 5- or 6-quart slow cooker. Cover and cook until lentils are tender, 2–3 hours on high or 4–6 hours on low.

2 At end of cooking time, stir in shrimp. Cover and cook on high until shrimp are just opaque in center, about 15 minutes.

♦ FILLING EXTRA

If you like, add 4 stalks of sliced celery instead of 2 in step 1. This recipe works with the Simply Filling technique.

PER SERVING (about 1³/₄ cups): 363 Cal, 3 g Fat, 0 g Sat Fat, 0 g Trans Fat, 336 mg Chol, 1,052 g Sod, 36 g Carb, 9 g Fib, 48 g Prot, 155 mg Calc. *POINTS* value: *7.*

Quinoa-and-Corn Stuffed Peppers

prep 20 min • slow-cook 2 hrs 20 min • serves 4

- 1/2 cup quinoa
- 1 (15-ounce) can black beans, rinsed and drained
- 2 cups packed baby spinach, coarsely chopped
- 1 cup fresh or thawed frozen corn kernels
- 1/2 cup crumbled fat-free feta cheese
- 2 scallions, chopped
- 1 1/2 teaspoons ground cumin
- 1 (14 1/2-ounce) can diced tomatoes
- 1/2 cup + 4 tablespoons fat-free green salsa
- 3 tablespoons chopped fresh cilantro
- 4 large assorted-color bell peppers, tops cut off

1 To make filling, cook quinoa according to package directions. Drain. Transfer to large bowl and let cool slightly, about 10 minutes.

2 Stir in beans, spinach, corn, feta, scallions, cumin, 1/4 cup tomatoes, 2 tablespoons salsa, and 2 tablespoons cilantro.

3 Spoon filling evenly into bell peppers. Transfer bell peppers, top side up, to 5- or 6-quart slow cooker. Combine remaining tomatoes and 1/2 cup + 2 tablespoons salsa in small bowl. Spoon tomato mixture over and around bell peppers. Cover and cook until bell peppers are fork-tender, 2–3 hours on high or 4–6 hours on low. Serve, sprinkled with remaining 1 tablespoon cilantro.

IN THE KITCHEN

To add extra-flavor to the quinoa filling, toast it first. Place the quinoa in a small skillet and set over medium-high heat. Toast, stirring frequently, until fragrant, about 3 minutes. This recipe works with the Simply Filling technique.

PER SERVING (1 stuffed pepper with 1/4 cup sauce): 318 Cal, 3 g Fat, 0 g Sat Fat, 0 g Trans Fat, 1 mg Chol, 823 mg Sod, 59 g Carb, 16 g Fib, 17 g Prot, 189 mg Calc. *POINTS* value: 6.

Bean and Sweet Potato Soup

prep 15 min • **cook/slow-cook** 4 hrs 5 min • **serves** 6

- 2   **teaspoons olive oil**
- ◆ 2   red onions, finely chopped
- 3   **garlic cloves, finely chopped**
- 1   **tablespoon curry powder**
- ◆ 1   (29-ounce) can black beans, rinsed and drained
- ◆ 1   (29-ounce) can red kidney beans, rinsed and drained
- ◆ 1   large sweet potato, peeled and diced
- $1/2$ **teaspoon salt**
- $1/4$ **teaspoon black pepper**
- ◆ 6   cups low-sodium vegetable broth
- ◆ $1/4$ cup plain fat-free yogurt
- 2   **tablespoons chopped fresh cilantro**

Grated zest of $1/2$ lime

1 Heat oil in large nonstick skillet over medium heat. Add onions and garlic; cook, stirring occasionally, until onion is softened, about 5 minutes. Add curry powder and cook, stirring constantly, until fragrant, about 30 seconds. Transfer onion mixture to 5- or 6-quart slow cooker. Stir in beans, potato, salt, and pepper. Pour broth over beans and vegetables. Cover and cook until vegetables are fork-tender, 4–5 hours on high or 8–10 hours on low.

2 Meanwhile, combine yogurt, cilantro, and lime zest in small bowl.

3 At end of cooking time, let mixture cool 10 minutes. Puree in batches in food processor or blender. Serve, topped with yogurt mixture.

This recipe works with the Simply Filling technique.

PER SERVING (2 cups and 1 scant tablespoon yogurt mixture): 322 Cal, 3 g Fat, 0 g Sat Fat, 0 g Trans Fat, 0 mg Chol, 1,083 mg Sod, 59 g Carb, 18 g Fib, 17 g Prot, 148 mg Calc. *POINTS* value: *6.*

Bulgur and Bean Chili

prep 20 min • cook/slow-cook 3 hrs 5 min • serves 6

- 1 tablespoon ground cumin
- ♦ 1 onion, chopped
- ♦ 2 assorted-color bell peppers, cut into 1-inch chunks
- ♦ 1 (20-ounce) bag peeled cut-up butternut squash, cut into 1-inch chunks
- ♦ 1 (15-ounce) can kidney beans, rinsed and drained
- ♦ 1 (15-ounce) can black beans, rinsed and drained
- ♦ 1 (14 1/2-ounce) can vegetable broth
- ♦ 1 (10-ounce) can diced tomatoes with green chiles
- ♦ 1 (8-ounce) can tomato sauce
- 3 garlic cloves, crushed through a press
- 1 tablespoon chili powder
- 1/4 teaspoon salt
- ♦ 1/2 cup bulgur
- ♦ 1 (9-ounce) box frozen cut green beans, thawed
- ♦ 3/4 cup shredded fat-free Monterey Jack cheese
- ♦ 1/3 cup fat-free sour cream

1 Set large nonstick skillet over medium heat. Add cumin and cook, stirring constantly, until toasted and fragrant, about 1 minute; transfer to 5- or 6-quart slow cooker.

2 Spray skillet with nonstick spray and set over medium heat. Add onion and cook, stirring occasionally, until softened, about 4 minutes. Transfer onion to slow cooker. Stir in bell peppers, squash, kidney beans, black beans, broth, diced tomatoes, tomato sauce, garlic, chili powder, and salt. Top vegetable mixture with bulgur, leaving 1/2-inch border from side of slow cooker. Cover and cook until bulgur and vegetables are fork-tender, 3–4 hours on high or 6–8 hours on low.

3 About 30 minutes before cooking time is up, stir in green beans. Cover and cook on high until green beans are just tender, about 25 minutes. Serve, topped with Monterey Jack and sour cream.

IN THE KITCHEN

If peeled cut-up butternut squash is not available at your supermarket, buy a 2-pound butternut squash and prep it yourself. The recipe works with the Simply Filling technique.

PER SERVING (about 1 3/4 cups chili with 2 tablespoons cheese and 1 scant tablespoon sour cream): 298 Cal, 2 g Fat, 0 g Sat Fat, 0 g Trans Fat, 4 mg Chol, 1,147 mg Sod, 58 g Carb, 15 g Fib, 17 g Prot, 291 mg Calc. *POINTS* value: *5.*

Three-Bean Chili

prep 15 min • **cook/slow-cook** 4 hrs • **serves** 4

- ◆ 1 large red onion, chopped
- ◆ 2 yellow bell peppers, diced
- ◆ 1 small rutabaga, peeled and diced
- ◆ 1 cup frozen baby lima beans, thawed
- ◆ 1 (15-ounce) can pinto beans, rinsed and drained
- ◆ 1 (15-ounce) can black beans, rinsed and drained
- ◆ 1 (15-ounce) can diced tomatoes in sauce
- ◆ 1 (8-ounce) can tomato sauce (no salt added)
- $1/3$ cup cayenne pepper sauce
- 2 tablespoons honey
- 3 tablespoons ancho chile powder
- 4 garlic cloves, coarsely chopped
- 1 tablespoon ground cumin
- 3 tablespoons shredded pepperjack cheese
- ◆ 2 scallions, sliced

Combine onion, bell peppers, rutabaga, lima beans, pinto beans, black beans, diced tomatoes, tomato sauce, pepper sauce, honey, chile powder, garlic, and cumin in 5- or 6-quart slow cooker. Cover and cook until vegetables are fork-tender, 4–5 hours on high or 8–10 hours on low. Serve, sprinkled with pepperjack and scallions.

IN THE KITCHEN
Don't let the amount of pepper sauce throw you in this recipe! Cayenne pepper sauce has a milder flavor than hot pepper sauce, which is made from fiery Tabasco peppers.

PER SERVING ($1^3/4$ cups chili with about 2 teaspoons cheese and $1/2$ tablespoon scallions): 324 Cal, 4 g Fat, 1 g Sat Fat, 0 g Trans Fat, 5 mg Chol, 1,000 mg Sod, 60 g Carb, 18 g Fib, 15 g Prot, 171 mg Calc. *POINTS* value: *6.*

Green Lentil Stew with Hot Spinach Salad

prep 15 min · slow-cook/cook 3 hrs 10 min · serves 6

- ◆ 3½ cups low-sodium chicken or vegetable broth
- ◆ 1½ cups dried green (French) lentils, picked over, rinsed, and drained
- ◆ 3 carrots, thinly sliced
- ◆ 3 celery stalks, sliced
- 3 **garlic cloves, minced**
- ◆ 2 tablespoons tomato paste
- ½ **teaspoon dried thyme**
- ½ **teaspoon salt**
- 2 **teaspoons olive oil**
- ◆ 1 large red onion, chopped
- 2 **tablespoons red-wine vinegar**
- 1 **teaspoon Dijon mustard**
- ⅛ **teaspoon black pepper**
- ◆ 1 (6-ounce) bag baby spinach

1 Combine broth, lentils, carrots, celery, garlic, tomato paste, thyme, and ¼ teaspoon salt in 5- or 6-quart slow cooker. Cover and cook until lentils are fork-tender, 3–4 hours on high or 6–8 hours on low.

2 At end of cooking time, heat oil in large nonstick skillet over medium heat. Add onion and cook, stirring frequently, until softened and lightly browned, about 8 minutes. Remove skillet from heat. Stir in vinegar, mustard, pepper, and remaining ¼ teaspoon salt. Return skillet to heat and cook just until vinegar comes to a simmer.

3 Put spinach in large bowl; add onion mixture and toss to combine. Serve with lentils.

IN THE KITCHEN
Green lentils are smaller than brown lentils, have a slightly peppery flavor, and hold their shape well. They can be found in some supermarkets, specialty food stores, or health food stores. This recipe works with the Simply Filling technique.

PER SERVING (generous 1 cup lentils with generous 1½ cups spinach mixture):
345 Cal, 5 g Fat, 1 g Sat Fat, 0 g Trans Fat, 0 mg Chol, 549 mg Sod, 55 g Carb, 15 g Fib, 25 g Prot, 135 mg Calc. *POINTS* value: *7.*

Lentil-Winter Squash Stew

prep 20 min • **cook/slow-cook** 4 hrs 20 min • **serves** 6

- ◆ 1¹/₂ cups dried lentils, picked over, rinsed, and drained
- ◆ 1 (15¹/₂-ounce) can chickpeas, rinsed and drained
- 2 tablespoons minced peeled fresh ginger
- 4 large garlic cloves, minced
- ¹/₄ teaspoon red pepper flakes
- ◆ 1³/₄ pounds buttercup or butternut squash, peeled, seeded and cut into 1-inch chunks
- ◆ 2¹/₂ cups vegetable broth
- ◆ 1 (14¹/₂-ounce) can Italian-style stewed tomatoes
- ◆ 1 (6-ounce) bag baby spinach
- ◆ 2 (10-ounce) bags frozen broccoli, cauliflower, carrot, and zucchini blend, thawed

1 Combine lentils, chickpeas, ginger, garlic, and red pepper flakes in 5- or 6-quart slow cooker. Top with squash. Pour broth into slow cooker. Cover and cook until lentils and squash are fork-tender, 4–5 hours on high or 8–10 hours on low.

2 About 20 minutes before cooking time is up, stir tomatoes and half of spinach into slow cooker. When spinach begins to wilt, after about 5 minutes, stir in remaining spinach. Cover and cook on high until spinach wilts completely, about 10 minutes.

3 At end of cooking time, stir vegetable blend into slow cooker. Cover and cook on high until vegetables are crisp-tender, about 20 minutes.

This recipe works with the Simply Filling technique.

PER SERVING (1¹/₂ cups): 306 Cal, 2 g Fat, 0 g Sat Fat, 0 g Trans Fat, 0 mg Chol, 741 mg Sod, 59 g Carb, 19 g Fib, 19 g Prot, 137 mg Calc. *POINTS* value: *5.*

Mixed-Grain Quick Bread

prep 20 min • **slow-cook** 2 hrs 30 min • **serves** 12

1 cup whole wheat flour
1 cup all-purpose flour
♦ $1/3$ cup old-fashioned oats
♦ $1/4$ cup cornmeal
2 tablespoons sunflower seeds
1 tablespoon millet (optional)
1 teaspoon baking powder
$3/4$ teaspoon salt
$1/4$ teaspoon baking soda
♦ $1 1/4$ cups fat-free buttermilk
♦ 1 large egg
2 tablespoons honey
1 tablespoon olive or canola oil

1 Spray $1 1/2$-quart soufflé dish with nonstick spray. Place small rack in bottom of 5- or 6-quart slow cooker.

2 Combine whole wheat flour, all-purpose flour, $1/4$ cup oats, cornmeal, sunflower seeds, millet (if using), baking powder, salt, and baking soda in large bowl. Whisk buttermilk, egg, honey, and oil in medium bowl. Add buttermilk mixture to flour mixture and stir just until flour mixture is moistened. Transfer dough to prepared dish and spread evenly. Sprinkle with remaining oats.

3 Spray 12-inch square of foil with nonstick spray. Cover dish tightly with foil, sprayed side down. Transfer dish to slow cooker. Pour 1 cup hot water around dish. Cover and cook until toothpick inserted into center of bread comes out clean, $2 1/2$–3 hours on high.

4 Transfer dish to another rack and let cool 10 minutes. Run thin knife around bread to loosen it from dish. Remove bread from dish and let cool completely on rack. Cut into 12 wedges.

♦ **FILLING EXTRA**
For a satisfying snack, toast a wedge of the bread and spread it with 2 tablespoons mashed avocado. The per-serving **POINTS** value will increase by **1**.

PER SERVING (1 wedge): 139 Cal, 3 g Fat, 1 g Sat Fat, 0 g Trans Fat, 19 mg Chol, 100 mg Sod, 24 g Carb, 2 g Fib, 5 g Prot, 62 mg Calc. *POINTS* value: **3**.

Spiced Apple-Nut Bread

prep 20 min • **slow-cook** 2 hrs 30 min • **serves** 12

- ♦ $^1/_2$ cup unsweetened applesauce
- ♦ 1 large egg
- ♦ 1 large egg white
- 2 tablespoons canola oil
- $1^1/_2$ cups white whole wheat flour
- $^1/_2$ cup packed brown sugar
- 1 teaspoon apple pie spice
- 1 teaspoon baking powder
- $^1/_2$ teaspoon salt
- $^1/_4$ teaspoon baking soda
- ♦ 1 Granny Smith apple, peeled and chopped
- 8 tablespoons walnuts, chopped

1 Spray $1^1/_2$-quart soufflé dish with nonstick spray. Place small rack in bottom of 5- or 6-quart slow cooker.

2 Whisk applesauce, egg, egg white, and oil in medium bowl. Combine flour, brown sugar, pie spice, baking powder, salt, and baking soda in large bowl, breaking up any lumps of sugar. Stir in applesauce mixture, apple, and 6 tablespoons walnuts just until flour mixture is moistened (dough will be stiff). Transfer dough to prepared dish and spread evenly. Sprinkle with remaining 2 tablespoons walnuts.

3 Spray 12-inch square of foil with nonstick spray. Cover dish tightly with foil, sprayed side down. Transfer dish to slow cooker. Pour 1 cup hot water around dish. Cover and cook until toothpick inserted into center of bread comes out clean, $2^1/_2$–3 hours on high.

4 Transfer dish to another rack and let cool 15 minutes. Run thin knife around bread to loosen it from dish. Remove bread from dish and let cool completely on rack. Cut into 12 wedges.

IN THE KITCHEN

Look for white whole wheat flour at the supermarket or health food store. It has all the fiber and nutrition of traditional whole wheat flour, but with a milder flavor and lighter color. Or substitute 1 cup whole wheat flour and $^1/_2$ cup all-purpose flour in this recipe.

PER SERVING (1 wedge): 154 Cal, 6 g Fat, 1 g Sat Fat, 0 g Trans Fat, 18 mg Chol, 179 mg Sod, 24 g Carb, 3 g Fib, 4 g Prot, 44 mg Calc. *POINTS* value: *3.*

VEGGIE-STUFFED ONIONS,
PAGE 162

Chapter 6

Vegetarian Main Dishes and Sides

Looking for new veggie ideas? Only 20 minutes prep (or less) is required—and the slow cooker does the rest!

Veggie-Stuffed Onions

prep 25 min • **slow-cook** 3 hrs • **serves** 4

- ◆ 4   (³/₄-pound each) Vidalia onions
- ◆ 1   (12-ounce) package frozen soy crumbles, thawed
- ◆ 1   cup cooked brown rice
- ◆ 1   (10-ounce) bag frozen peas and carrots, thawed

    Grated zest and juice of ¹/₂ lemon

- 1   teaspoon dried sage
- ¹/₂   teaspoon salt
- ¹/₂   teaspoon black pepper
- ¹/₄   teaspoon ground allspice
- ◆ 2   cups tomato puree (no salt added)
- ◆ ¹/₂   cup low-sodium chicken broth
- 3   tablespoons chopped fresh dill
- 1   tablespoon Worcestershire sauce

1 Trim bottom of each onion to stand onions upright, making sure bottoms are left intact to hold filling. Trim little more than ¹/₄ inch from top of each onion. With melon baller, or small sharp knife, cut out onion centers, leaving all but outer layer. Discard onion centers (or chop and freeze for another use).

2 To make filling, combine soy crumbles, rice, 1 cup peas and carrots, lemon zest, sage, salt, pepper, and allspice in medium bowl. Fill onion cavities evenly with filling, packing firmly. Transfer onions to 5- or 6-quart slow cooker. Sprinkle remaining peas and carrots around onions.

3 Mix tomato puree, broth, lemon juice, 2 tablespoons dill, and Worcestershire sauce in medium bowl; pour around onions (not over tops). Cover and cook until onions are fork-tender, 3–4 hours on high or 6–8 hours on low. Serve, sprinkled with remaining 1 tablespoon dill.

IN THE KITCHEN

If the outer layer of an onion is too thin when cutting out the center in step 1, leave 2 layers so it doesn't collapse while cooking.

PER SERVING (1 stuffed onion with ¹/₂ cup sauce): 313 Cal, 2 g Fat, 0 g Sat Fat, 0 g Trans Fat, 0 mg Chol, 447 mg Sod, 42 g Carb, 9 g Fib, 35 g Prot, 127 mg Calc. *POINTS* value: *6.*

Thai Tempeh with Vegetables

prep 15 min • **slow-cook/cook** 3 hrs 5 min • **serves** 4

♦ 3/4 pound small red potatoes, scrubbed and quartered

♦ 1 (8-ounce) package tempeh, cut into 1/2-inch cubes

♦ 2 cups baby carrots

♦ 2 cups fresh cauliflower florets

♦ 1 small tomato, diced

♦ 1 small onion, thinly sliced

1/2 cup light coconut milk

3 garlic cloves, minced

2 tablespoons unsweetened shredded coconut

1/4 cup chutney

1 Combine potatoes, tempeh, carrots, cauliflower, tomato, onion, coconut milk, and garlic in 5- or 6-quart slow cooker. Cover and cook until vegetables are fork-tender, 3–4 hours on high or 6–8 hours on low.

2 Meanwhile spread coconut in small nonstick skillet and set over medium-high heat. Cook, stirring frequently, until lightly browned, about 5 minutes. Let cool.

3 At end of cooking time, stir chutney into stew until blended. Serve, sprinkled with coconut.

♦ **FILLING EXTRA**

Add peas to this mild Thai stew. Prepare the recipe as directed but 20 minutes before the end of the cooking time, stir in 2 cups thawed frozen peas. Cover and cook on high until the peas are heated through, about 15 minutes. Increase the per-serving *POINTS* value by *1.*

PER SERVING (1 1/4 cups): 281 Cal, 10 g Fat, 4 g Sat Fat, 0 g Trans Fat, 0 mg Chol, 116 mg Sod, 39 g Carb, 8 g Fib, 15 g Prot, 128 mg Calc. *POINTS value: 6.*

Tofu Vegetable Stew

prep 15 min • slow-cook 3 hrs • serves 4

- 1 pound extra-firm tofu, cut into 1-inch cubes
- 2 cups low-sodium vegetable broth or water
- 4 large carrots, thinly sliced
- 1 large red onion, chopped
- 6 ounces shiitake mushrooms, stems discarded and quartered
- 2 tablespoons low-sodium soy sauce
- 1 teaspoon Asian (dark) sesame oil
- 2 cups thinly sliced Napa cabbage
- 1/2 cup water
- 3 tablespoons miso
- 2 scallions, thinly sliced

1 Combine tofu, broth, carrots, onion, mushrooms, soy sauce, and sesame oil in 5- or 6-quart slow cooker. Cover and cook until vegetables are fork-tender, 3–4 hours on high or 6–8 hours on low.

2 About 35 minutes before cooking time is up, stir cabbage into slow cooker. Cover and cook on high until cabbage is crisp-tender, about 30 minutes.

3 At end of cooking time, whisk water and miso in small bowl until smooth. Stir miso mixture into stew. Serve, sprinkled with scallions.

◆ FILLING EXTRA

Keep an 8.8-ounce bag of shelf-stable cooked brown rice on hand for saucy stews like this one. It reheats in the microwave in just 90 seconds. A 1/2 cup of cooked brown rice per serving will increase the **POINTS** value by **2.**

PER SERVING (1 1/2 cups): 216 Cal, 9 g Fat, 1 g Sat Fat, 0 g Trans Fat, 0 mg Chol, 976 mg Sod, 22 g Carb, 6 g Fib, 16 g Prot, 285 mg Calc.
POINTS value: *4.*

Barbecue Tofu Chili

prep 20 min • **slow-cook** 4 hrs • **serves** 4

- ♦ 2½ cups peeled and diced acorn squash
- ♦ 1 (10-ounce) package sliced cremini mushrooms
- ♦ 2 celery stalks, chopped
- ♦ 1 large red onion, chopped
- ♦ 1 poblano pepper, diced
- ♦ 1 (14½-ounce) can diced tomatoes with roasted garlic
- ♦ 1 (15-ounce) can black beans, rinsed and drained
- 3 tablespoons cayenne pepper sauce
- ♦ 3 tablespoons tomato paste
- 3 tablespoons ancho chile powder
- 2 tablespoons honey
- 1 tablespoon ground cumin
- 2 teaspoons dried oregano
- 2 (6-ounce) packages barbecue-flavored tofu, cut into ¾-inch cubes
- ♦ 2 tablespoons cornmeal
- 3 tablespoons shredded low-fat Monterey Jack cheese

1 Combine squash, mushrooms, celery, onion, poblano, tomatoes, beans, pepper sauce, tomato paste, chile powder, honey, cumin, and oregano in 5- or 6-quart slow cooker. Press vegetables down into tomato mixture to form even layer. Top with tofu, leaving 1-inch border from side of slow cooker. Cover and cook until vegetables are fork-tender, 4–5 hours on high or 8–10 hours on low.

2 About 20 minutes before cooking time is up, gradually stir cornmeal into slow cooker until blended. Cover and cook on high until mixture simmers and thickens, about 15 minutes. Serve, sprinkled with Monterey Jack.

♦ **FILLING EXTRA**
Serve each portion of this hearty chili topped with 2 tablespoons of your favorite fat-free salsa.

PER SERVING (2 cups chili with about 2 teaspoons cheese): 329 Cal, 7 g Fat, 1 g Sat Fat, 0 g Trans Fat, 3 mg Chol, 1,129 mg Sod, 56 g Carb, 12 g Fib, 18 g Prot, 323 mg Calc. *POINTS* value: **6.**

"Sausage"-Stuffed Eggplant

prep 15 min • cook/slow-cook 3 hrs 5 min • serves 4

- ◆ 1 (1¼-pound) eggplant, halved lengthwise
-   2 teaspoons extra-virgin olive oil
- ◆ 1 large onion, chopped
-   ¼ pound frozen vegetarian sausage patties, chopped
-   2 garlic cloves, minced
- ◆ 1 cup cooked brown rice
-   2 tablespoons chopped fresh dill
-   2 tablespoons chopped fresh mint
-   ½ teaspoon salt
-   ½ teaspoon coarsely ground black pepper
- ◆ 1 (8-ounce) can tomato sauce
-   ¼ cup crumbled low-fat feta cheese

1 With grapefruit spoon, scoop out flesh from each eggplant half leaving ½-inch shell. Coarsely chop scooped flesh and set aside.

2 To make stuffing, heat oil in large nonstick skillet over medium-high heat. Add onion, sausage, chopped eggplant, and garlic; cook, stirring frequently, until onion is softened, about 3 minutes. Remove skillet from heat. Stir in rice, dill, mint, salt, and pepper.

3 Fill each eggplant shell with half of stuffing. Transfer stuffed halves to 5- or 6-quart slow cooker. Top with tomato sauce. Cover and cook until eggplant and filling are fork-tender, 3–4 hours on high or 6–8 hours on low. Serve, sprinkled with feta.

IN THE KITCHEN

To make the eggplant flesh easier to scoop out, score the cut side of each eggplant half with a small sharp knife, taking care not to pierce the skin.

PER SERVING (¼ stuffed eggplant with about 2 tablespoons sauce and 1 tablespoon cheese): 224 Cal, 7 g Fat, 1 g Sat Fat, 0 g Trans Fat, 3 mg Chol, 849 mg Sod, 33 g Carb, 7 g Fib, 11 g Prot, 86 mg Calc. *POINTS* value: *4.*

Cheese and Spinach–Stuffed Savoy Cabbage

prep 20 min • microwave/slow-cook 3 hrs 5 min • serves 4

- ◆ 8   large Savoy cabbage leaves
- 1   (15-ounce) container low-fat ricotta cheese
- ◆ 1¹/₂ cups baby spinach, chopped
- ¹/₄   pound shallots, minced
- ¹/₄   cup chopped fresh parsley
- ◆ 1   large egg
- 4   tablespoons grated pecorino cheese
- ¹/₂   teaspoon salt
- ¹/₄   teaspoon black pepper
- ◆ 1   (8-ounce) can tomato sauce
- 2   tablespoons chopped fresh basil

1 Spread cabbage leaves on large microwavable plate and cover with paper towel. Microwave on High until softened, 3–4 minutes. Transfer leaves to cutting board. When cool enough to handle, trim thick ribs from leaves.

2 Meanwhile, to make filling, mix ricotta, spinach, shallots, parsley, egg, 2 tablespoons pecorino, salt, and pepper.

3 Place ¹/₃ cup filling on center of each cabbage leaf. Fold in sides and roll up. Transfer rolls, seam side down, to 5- or 6-quart slow cooker. Top with tomato sauce. Cover and cook until cabbage is fork-tender, 3–4 hours on high or 6–8 hours on low. Serve, sprinkled with basil and remaining 2 tablespoons pecorino.

IN THE KITCHEN

To remove the cabbage leaves from the head of cabbage, cut around the core of the cabbage with a small sharp knife (it's not necessary to remove the core). Carefully peel off each leaf, one at a time, taking not to tear them.

PER SERVING (2 rolls with 2 tablespoons sauce and ¹/₂ tablespoon each basil and cheese): 225 Cal, 11 g Fat, 6 g Sat Fat, 0 g Trans Fat, 88 mg Chol, 795 mg Sod, 17 g Carb, 3 g Fib, 17 g Prot, 373 mg Calc. *POINTS* value: 5.

Broccoflower and Cheese Soup

prep 20 min • **roast/slow-cook** 4 hrs 30 min • **serves** 4

♦ 1   head broccoflower, cored and cut into 1-inch pieces

♦ 2   medium red onions, chopped

♦ 3   carrots, chopped

2   **teaspoons olive oil**

1   **teaspoon dried thyme**

¼   **teaspoon salt**

¼   **teaspoon black pepper**

♦ 1   (32-ounce) carton vegetable broth

½   **cup coarsely shredded low-fat Cheddar cheese**

1 Preheat oven to 450°F. Combine broccoflower, onions, carrots, oil, and thyme in large bowl. Transfer vegetables to large rimmed baking sheet and spread in single layer. Roast until lightly browned, about 30 minutes, stirring vegetables every 10 minutes. Transfer vegetables to 5- or 6-quart slow cooker. Add salt and pepper. Pour broth over vegetable mixture. Cover and cook until vegetables are fork-tender, 4–5 hours on high or 8–10 hours on low.

2 At end of cooking time, let mixture cool 5 minutes. Puree in batches in food processor or blender. Serve, topped with Cheddar.

♦ **FILLING EXTRA**

For a creamier soup, add 1 cup fat-free ricotta cheese to the soup mixture before pureeing it in step 2. The per-serving **POINTS** value will increase by **1**.

PER SERVING (2 cups soup with 2 tablespoons cheese): 206 Cal, 9 g Fat, 4 g Sat Fat, 0 g Trans Fat, 18 mg Chol, 516 mg Sod, 22 g Carb, 6 g Fib, 14 g Prot, 214 mg Calc. **POINTS** value: **4**.

Cauliflower and Lentils with Feta

prep 15 min • slow-cook 1 hr 30 min • serves 4

♦ 1   (1½-pound) cauliflower, cut into 2-inch florets

♦ 1   large yellow onion, chopped

♦ ½   cup vegetable or chicken broth

3   garlic cloves, chopped

1   teaspoon ground cumin

1   teaspoon salt

⅛   teaspoon cayenne

♦ 1   (8-ounce) package cooked black Beluga lentils or 1½ cups cooked green (French) lentils

1   cup crumbled low-fat feta cheese

1   lime, cut into 4 wedges

1 Combine cauliflower, onion, broth, garlic, cumin, salt, and cayenne in 5- or 6-quart slow cooker. Cover and cook until cauliflower is just tender, 1½–2 hours on high or 3–4 hours on low.

2 About 15 minutes before cooking time is up, stir lentils into slow cooker. Cover and cook on high until heated through, about 10 minutes.

3 At end of cooking time, sprinkle cauliflower and lentil mixture with feta. Serve with lime wedges.

IN THE KITCHEN

Black beluga lentils (which look like caviar after cooking, hence the name) are one of the smallest varieties of the lentil family. Like green lentils, they hold their shape well after cooking and are terrific hot and in salads.

PER SERVING (1 cup cauliflower and lentils with ¼ cup cheese and 1 lime wedge): 187 Cal, 4 g Fat, 2 g Sat Fat, 0 g Trans Fat, 12 mg Chol, 1,170 mg Sod, 28 g Carb, 7 g Fib, 13 g Prot, 193 mg Calc. POINTS value: 3.

Greens and Black-Eyed Peas

prep 10 min • slow-cook 3 hrs • serves 4

♦ 2   cups frozen black-eyed peas, thawed

♦ 1   cup vegetable broth or water

♦ 1   large onion, chopped

♦ 1   celery stalk, diced

3   garlic cloves, minced

1/2   teaspoon salt

1/2   teaspoon dried thyme

1/2   teaspoon ground allspice

1/4   teaspoon red pepper flakes

♦ 3/4   pound collard greens, stems discarded and leaves sliced 1/2 inch thick

♦ 2   cups hot cooked brown rice

1 Combine black-eyed peas, broth, onion, celery, garlic, salt, thyme, allspice, and red pepper flakes in 5- or 6-quart slow cooker. Cover and cook until vegetables are fork-tender, 3–4 hours on high or 6–8 hours on low.

2 About 35 minutes before cooking time is up, stir greens into slow cooker. Cover and cook on high until greens are crisp-tender, about 30 minutes. Serve with rice.

♦ FILLING EXTRA

Add 2 chopped carrots with the vegetables in step 1. This recipe works with the Simply Filling technique.

PER SERVING (1 cup black-eyed peas and greens with 1/2 cup rice): 263 Cal, 2 g Fat, 0 g Sat Fat, 0 g Trans Fat, 0 mg Chol, 562 mg Sod, 52 g Carb, 12 g Fib, 12 g Prot, 143 mg Calc. *POINTS* value: *5.*

Veggie and Bean Chipotle Chili

prep 15 min • **slow-cook** 4 hrs • **serves** 4

- ◆ 1 (15-ounce) can pinto beans, rinsed and drained
- ◆ 1 (14½-ounce) can diced tomatoes in sauce
- ◆ 1 (8-ounce) can Italian-style tomato sauce
- ◆ 1 (8-ounce) package cremini mushrooms, halved
- ◆ 2 large yellow bell peppers, diced
- ◆ 1 large red onion, chopped
- 2½ tablespoons chipotle chile powder
- 1 tablespoon packed brown sugar
- ½ teaspoon salt
- ◆ 1 pound zucchini, cut into 1-inch chunks
- ◆ 2 tablespoons cornmeal
- ¼ cup low-fat Greek yogurt

1 Combine beans, diced tomatoes, tomato sauce, mushrooms, bell peppers, onion, chile powder, brown sugar, and salt in 5- or 6-quart slow cooker. Press vegetables down into tomato mixture to form even layer. Top with zucchini. Cover and cook until vegetables are fork-tender, 4–5 hours on high or 8–10 hours on low.

2 About 20 minutes before cooking time is up, gradually stir cornmeal into slow cooker until blended. Cover and cook on high until mixture simmers and thickens, about 15 minutes. Serve with yogurt.

◆ **FILLING EXTRA**
Microwave 2 (6-ounce) baking potatoes until fork-tender. Split the potatoes, then spoon each serving of chili over a potato half (and up the *POINTS* value by *1*).

PER SERVING (about 1¾ cups with 1 tablespoon yogurt): 290 Cal, 2 g Fat, 1 g Sat Fat, 0 g Trans Fat, 1 mg Chol, 926 mg Sod, 59 g Carb, 13 g Fib, 14 g Prot, 168 mg Calc. *POINTS* value: *5.*

Minestrone

prep 15 min • slow-cook/cook 4 hrs • serves 6

- ♦ 1 (15 ½-ounce) can Navy beans, rinsed and drained
- ♦ 2 carrots, diced
- ♦ 2 baking potatoes, peeled and diced
- ♦ 2 red onions, chopped
- ♦ 2 small yellow squash, diced
- ♦ ½ fennel bulb, chopped
- ♦ ¼ pound fresh green beans, trimmed and cut into 1-inch pieces
- 10 fresh flat-leaf parsley sprigs
- 2 garlic cloves, peeled
- ½ teaspoon salt
- ¼ teaspoon black pepper
- ♦ 1 (32-ounce) carton vegetable broth
- 1 cup orzo

1 Combine Navy beans, carrots, potatoes, onions, squash, fennel, green beans, parsley, garlic, salt, and pepper in 5- or 6-quart slow cooker. Pour broth over beans and vegetables. Cover and cook until vegetables are fork-tender, 4–5 hours on high or 8–10 hours on low.

2 About 20 minutes before cooking time is up, cook orzo according to package directions, omitting salt if desired.

3 At end of cooking time, discard parsley and garlic. Gently stir orzo into slow cooker.

♦ FILLING EXTRA

Add 2 peeled and diced parsnips to the slow cooker with the beans and vegetables in step 1.

PER SERVING (2 cups): 211 Cal, 3 g Fat, 1 g Sat Fat, 0 g Trans Fat, 5 mg Chol, 465 mg Sod, 40 g Carb, 7 g Fib, 11 g Prot, 85 mg Calc. *POINTS* value: *4.*

White Vegetable Soup

prep 20 min • **slow-cook** 3 hrs 5 min • **serves** 4

- ½ pound leeks, cleaned and chopped, white and light green parts only
- 2 garlic cloves, chopped
- 1 pound celeriac, peeled and chopped
- 1 pound parsnips, peeled and chopped
- ½ pound turnips, peeled and chopped
- ½ teaspoon dried thyme
- ½ teaspoon salt
- 3 cups vegetable or chicken broth
- ½ cup fat-free milk
- ¼ teaspoon Aleppo pepper or pinch cayenne

1 Combine leeks, garlic, celeriac, parsnips, turnips, thyme, and salt in 5- or 6-quart slow cooker. Stir in broth. Cover and cook until vegetables are fork-tender, 3–4 hours on high or 6–8 hours on low.

2 At end of cooking time, uncover and let mixture cool 5 minutes. Puree in batches in blender. Return puree to slow cooker; stir in milk and Aleppo pepper. Cover and cook on high until soup is heated through, about 5 minutes.

IN THE KITCHEN

Aleppo pepper is chile powder from Turkey. It's similar in taste to ancho chile powder, but with a little more heat and tartness. This recipe works with the Simply Filling technique.

PER SERVING (1½ cups): 170 Cal, 1 g Fat, 0 g Sat Fat, 0 g Trans Fat, 1 mg Chol, 1,172 mg Sod, 39 g Carb, 8 g Fib, 5 g Prot, 160 mg Calc. *POINTS* value: *3.*

Squash and Cranberry Soup with Yogurt Drizzle

prep 20 min • **slow-cook** 4 hrs 5 min • **serves** 4

- 1½ pounds butternut or kabocha squash, peeled, seeded, and cut into 1-inch chunks
- 2 Granny Smith apples, peeled and chopped
- 1 large onion, chopped
- 1 cup fresh or thawed frozen cranberries
- 1 cup unsweetened apple juice
- 1 cup water
- 1 tablespoon minced peeled fresh ginger
- 2 teaspoons extra-virgin olive oil
- ½ teaspoon salt
- ½ cup plain fat-free yogurt
- 1 tablespoon maple syrup

Pinch black pepper

1 Combine squash, apples, onion, cranberries, apple juice, water, ginger, oil, and salt in 5- or 6-quart slow cooker. Cover and cook until vegetables are fork-tender, 4–5 hours on high or 8–10 hours on low.

2 At end of cooking time, uncover and let mixture cool 5 minutes. Puree in batches in blender. Return puree to slow cooker. Cover and cook on high until soup is heated through, about 5 minutes.

3 Meanwhile, mix yogurt, maple syrup, and pepper in small bowl. Divide soup among 4 bowls. Serve, drizzled with yogurt mixture.

IN THE KITCHEN

Love ginger? Add another tablespoon of minced peeled fresh ginger to the soup before you puree it in step 2.

PER SERVING (1 cup soup with 1½ tablespoons yogurt mixture): 198 Cal, 3 g Fat, 0 g Sat Fat, 0 g Trans Fat, 1 mg Chol, 331 mg Sod, 44 g Carb, 5 g Fib, 4 g Prot, 137 mg Calc. *POINTS* value: 3.

Leeks with Dill Sauce

prep 10 min • low-cook/cook 3 hrs 5 min • serves 4

♦ 8 (10- to 12-inch) trimmed and cleaned whole leeks

♦ 1/4 cup vegetable broth

1 tablespoon unsalted butter

3/4 teaspoon salt

♦ 1 large egg

Juice of 1 small lemon

1 tablespoon chopped fresh dill

1/4 teaspoon black pepper

1 Combine leeks, broth, butter, and 1/2 teaspoon salt in 5- or 6-quart slow cooker. Cover and cook until leeks are fork-tender, 3–4 hours on high or 6–8 hours on low.

2 At end of cooking time, transfer leeks with slotted spoon to platter; cover and keep warm.

3 Whisk egg, lemon juice, dill, and pepper in small bowl. Pour hot liquid from slow cooker into small saucepan. Cook over medium heat until liquid comes to a simmer, about 2 minutes. Remove saucepan from heat. Slowly pour in egg mixture, whisking constantly. Return saucepan to heat and cook, whisking constantly, until sauce is thickened, about 1 minute. Pour sauce over leeks.

IN THE KITCHEN

Cook 4 frozen vegetarian patties according to the package directions to serve alongside this elegant vegetable dish (and up the per-serving *POINTS* value by *2).

PER SERVING (2 leeks with 2 tablespoons sauce): 156 Cal, 5 g Fat, 3 g Sat Fat, 0 g Trans Fat, 61 mg Chol, 552 mg Sod, 26 g Carb, 3 g Fib, 4 g Prot, 114 mg Calc. *POINTS* value: *3.*

Vegetable Sancocho

prep 15 min • **slow-cook** 2 hrs • **serves** 4

6	garlic cloves, chopped
◆ 1	(½-pound) yucca, peeled and cut into 2-inch chunks
◆ ½	pound red potatoes, scrubbed and halved
◆ ½	pound acorn squash or fresh pumpkin, peeled, seeded, and cut into 2-inch chunks
◆ 1	large red onion, thinly sliced
◆ 1	red bell pepper, cut into 1-inch chunks
◆ 1	cup canned diced tomatoes
1	cup water
1	teaspoon kosher salt
½	teaspoon dried oregano
◆ 2	ears corn on the cob, husked and cut crosswise into 2-inch pieces
¼	cup chopped fresh cilantro
1	tablespoon red-wine vinegar
	Hot pepper sauce (optional)

1 Set aside 2 teaspoons garlic. Combine yucca, potatoes, squash, onion, bell pepper, tomatoes, water, salt, oregano, and remaining garlic in 5- or 6-quart slow cooker. Cover and cook until vegetables are fork-tender, 2–3 hours on high or 4–6 hours on low.

2 About 35 minutes before cooking time is up, stir corn into slow cooker. Cover and cook on high until corn is fork-tender, about 30 minutes.

3 Just before serving, stir reserved 2 teaspoons garlic, cilantro, and vinegar into slow cooker. Serve with pepper sauce (if using).

IN THE KITCHEN

Sancocho, a traditional Latin American stew, usually includes large pieces of meat as well as vegetables. But our vegetarian version is equally satisfying. Serve this dish with 2⅔ cups cooked whole wheat couscous (⅔ cup cooked couscous per serving will up the **POINTS** value by **2**). This recipe works with the Simply Filling technique.

PER SERVING (1½ cups): 231 Cal, 1 g Fat, 0 g Sat Fat, 0 g Trans Fat, 0 mg Chol, 495 mg Sod, 53 g Carb, 8 g Fib, 6 g Prot, 122 mg Calc. *POINTS* value: *4*.

Fennel and Onions with Saffron

prep 10 min • cook/slow-cook 3 hrs 15 min • serves 4

2 teaspoons extra-virgin olive oil

♦ 2 fennel bulbs, quartered

♦ 4 small onions, each halved through the root end

♦ 1/2 cup low-sodium chicken broth or water

1 teaspoon kosher salt

1/2 teaspoon ground coriander

1/4 teaspoon black pepper

Pinch saffron

♦ 1 plum tomato, seeded and chopped

1 Heat 1 teaspoon oil in large nonstick skillet over medium-high heat. Add enough of fennel (about two thirds) so that it fits in single layer and cook until browned, 3–4 minutes per side. Transfer fennel to 5- or 6-quart slow cooker. Heat remaining 1 teaspoon oil in skillet. Add single layer of remaining fennel and onions; cook until browned, 3–4 minutes per side. Transfer fennel and onions to slow cooker.

2 Add broth to skillet and bring to boil, scraping up browned bits from bottom of pan. Stir broth mixture, salt, coriander, pepper, and saffron into slow cooker. Cover and cook until vegetables are fork-tender, 3–4 hours on high or 6–8 hours on low. Serve warm or at room temperature sprinkled with tomato.

IN THE KITCHEN

In addition to the tomato, top this dish with a combination of 2 tablespoons coarsely chopped fennel fronds or fresh basil and the grated zest of 1/2 small lemon. This recipe works with the Simply Filling technique.

PER SERVING (1 1/2 cups): 93 Cal, 3 g Fat, 0 g Sat Fat, 0 g Trans Fat, 0 mg Chol, 469 mg Sod, 16 g Carb, 5 g Fib, 3 g Prot, 79 mg Calc. *POINTS* value: *1.*

Chayote with Five-Spice Sauce

prep 10 min • cook/slow-cook 2 hrs 5 min • serves 4

♦ 2 chayote, each quartered through root end

¹⁄₄ cup water

1 tablespoon sherry or vegetable broth

1 tablespoon soy sauce

1 tablespoon packed brown sugar

2 garlic cloves, minced

2 teaspoons minced peeled fresh ginger

¹⁄₄ teaspoon five-spice powder

¹⁄₄ teaspoon black pepper

¹⁄₂ teaspoon cornstarch

1 Combine chayote, water, sherry, soy sauce, brown sugar, garlic, ginger, five-spice powder, and pepper in 5- or 6-quart slow cooker. Cover and cook until chayote is fork-tender, 2–3 hours on high or 4–6 hours on low.

2 Transfer chayote with slotted spoon to plate; cover and keep warm. Pour hot liquid from slow cooker into small saucepan; whisk in cornstarch until smooth. Cook over medium-high heat, stirring occasionally, until mixture comes to boil. Cook, stirring occasionally, just until thickened, about 1 minute. Pour sauce over chayote.

IN THE KITCHEN

Pale green, pear-shaped chayote is a popular vegetable in Asian and Latin American cuisines. Its taste and texture are between that of a cucumber and an apple.

PER SERVING (2 pieces chayote with 1 tablespoon sauce): 50 Cal, 1 g Fat, 0 g Sat Fat, 0 g Trans Fat, 0 mg Chol, 79 mg Sod, 11 g Carb, 3 g Fib, 1 g Prot, 24 mg Calc. *POINTS* value: *0.*

Lemon-Glazed Carrots and Parsnips

prep 15 min • slow-cook/cook 2 hrs 5 min • serves 4

- 1   pound parsnips, peeled and cut matchstick strips
- 1   pound baby carrots

  Grated zest and juice of 1 lemon

  2   tablespoons mirin or other rice wine, such as sake

  2   tablespoons water

  1/2   teaspoon salt

1 Combine parsnips, carrots, lemon juice, mirin, water, and salt in 5- or 6-quart slow cooker. Cover and cook until vegetables are fork-tender, 2–3 hours on high or 4–6 hours on low.

2 Transfer vegetables with slotted spoon to plate; cover and keep warm. Pour hot liquid from slow cooker into small saucepan and bring to boil. Reduce heat and simmer until liquid becomes syrupy glaze, 3–4 minutes. Pour glaze over vegetables. Sprinkle with lemon zest and toss to blend.

◆ FILLING EXTRA
Add 1 turnip, peeled and cut into matchstick strips, along with the carrots and parsnips in step 1.

PER SERVING (generous 1 cup): 126 Cal, 1 g Fat, 0 g Sat Fat, 0 g Trans Fat, 0 mg Chol, 386 mg Sod, 30 g Carb, 8 g Fib, 2 g Prot, 77 mg Calc.
POINTS value: *2.*

Beets with Dried Cherries

prep 10 min • **slow-cook** 1 hr • **serves** 4

♦ 1   pound beets, trimmed, peeled, and cut into 1-inch chunks

¼   **pound shallots, thinly sliced**

⅓   **cup orange juice**

1   **bay leaf**

½   **teaspoon dried thyme or herbes de Provence**

½   **teaspoon salt**

2   **tablespoons dried cherries**

1   **teaspoon red-wine vinegar**

1   **tablespoon chopped fresh parsley**

¼   **teaspoon black pepper**

1 Combine beets, shallots, orange juice, bay leaf, thyme, and salt in 5- or 6-quart slow cooker. Cover and cook until beets are fork-tender, 1–2 hours on high or 2–4 hours on low.

2 About 10 minutes before cooking time is up, stir cherries into slow cooker. Cover and cook on high until cherries are softened, about 5 minutes. Discard bay leaf. Stir in vinegar, parsley, and pepper. Serve warm or at room temperature.

IN THE KITCHEN

To peel raw beets most easily, use a swivel-blade peeler. Also wear plastic gloves and an apron, so your hands and clothing won't turn beet red.

PER SERVING (¾ cup): 80 Cal, 0 g Fat, 0 g Sat Fat, 0 g Trans Fat, 0 mg Chol, 359 mg Sod, 18 g Carb, 3 g Fib, 2 g Prot, 33 mg Calc. *POINTS* value: *1.*

Green Beans Olivada

- 1 pound fresh green beans, trimmed
- 1 cup cherry tomatoes, halved
- 1 small onion, thinly sliced
- 3 garlic cloves, thinly sliced
- 10 brine-cured Kalamata olives, pitted and chopped
- 1/4 cup water
- 1/2 teaspoon salt
- 1/4 teaspoon black pepper
- 1/4 teaspoon dried thyme
- 1 tablespoon chopped fresh basil

Combine green beans, tomatoes, onion, garlic, olives, water, salt, pepper, and thyme in 5- or 6-quart slow cooker. Cover and cook until green beans are fork-tender, 2–3 hours on high or 4–6 hours on low. Serve, sprinkled with basil.

FILLING EXTRA
If you like, toss these Mediterranean-inspired green beans with 4 cups cooked whole wheat penne and up the per-serving **POINTS** value by **3.** This recipe works with the Simply Filling technique.

PER SERVING (1 cup): 62 Cal, 1 g Fat, 0 g Sat Fat, 0 g Trans Fat, 0 mg Chol, 392 mg Sod, 12 g Carb, 5 g Fib, 3 g Prot, 62 mg Calc. *POINTS* value: *1.*

APRICOT-ALMOND CRISP,
PAGE 189

Chapter 7

Easy Sweets

Thanks to the slow cooker, these foolproof cakes, cobblers, and puddings practically cook themselves.

Carrot Cake

prep 15 min • **slow-cook** 1 hr 30 min • **serves** 12

1 cup all-purpose flour

1/2 cup whole wheat flour

1 teaspoon baking powder

1/2 teaspoon baking soda

1 teaspoon cinnamon

1/2 teaspoon ground nutmeg

3/4 cup granulated sugar

1/3 cup canola oil

1/4 cup water

♦ 3/4 cup fat-free egg substitute

2 teaspoons vanilla extract

♦ 3 cups coarsely shredded carrots

1 cup raisins

1 tablespoon confectioners' sugar

1 Preheat heating base of 3 1/2- or 4-quart slow cooker to high. Spray stoneware with nonstick spray. Line bottom with wax paper and lightly spray paper with nonstick spray.

2 Whisk all purpose flour, whole wheat flour, baking powder, baking soda, cinnamon, and nutmeg in medium bowl. With electric mixer on medium-high speed, beat granulated sugar, oil, water, egg substitute, and 1 teaspoon vanilla about 2 minutes. Reduce speed to low, add flour mixture, and beat just until blended. Stir in carrots and raisins. Pour batter into stoneware and place it in heating base. Cover slow cooker with 2 double layers paper towels; then place lid on top. Cook until toothpick inserted into center of cake comes out clean, 1 1/2–2 hours.

3 Transfer stoneware to rack and let cool 15 minutes. Run thin knife around cake to loosen it from stoneware. Invert onto rack; remove wax paper. Let cool completely. Serve dusted with confectioners' sugar.

IN THE KITCHEN

Placing several layers of paper towels between the top of the slow cooker and the lid absorbs excess steam while the cake cooks. The result? A pleasantly moist-textured cake.

PER SERVING (1/12 of cake): 219 Cal, 6 g Fat, 1 g Sat Fat, 0 g Trans Fat, 0 mg Chol, 152 mg Sod, 38 g Carb, 2 g Fib, 5 g Prot, 69 mg Calc. *POINTS* value: 4.

Lemon Sponge Pudding with Blueberries

prep 15 min • **slow-cook** 2 hrs • **serves** 6

½ cup granulated sugar

3 tablespoons all-purpose flour

1 cup low-fat (1%) milk

Grated zest and juice of 2 large lemons

♦ 3 large eggs, separated

1 tablespoon unsalted butter, melted

¼ teaspoon salt

1 tablespoon confectioners' sugar

♦ 1 (6-ounce) container fresh blueberries

1 Preheat heating base of 5- or 6-quart slow cooker to high.

2 Combine granulated sugar and flour in medium bowl. Whisk in milk, lemon zest and juice, egg yolks, and melted butter. With electric mixer on high speed, beat egg whites and salt until stiff peaks form. With rubber spatula, gently fold beaten whites into lemon mixture just until no streaks of white remain.

3 Pour mixture into 2-quart glass bowl. Cover bowl tightly with foil, securing foil with rubber band. Place bowl in stoneware and place it in heating base; pour enough boiling water into stoneware to come halfway up outside of bowl. Cover and cook until top is set, about 2 hours.

4 Carefully transfer bowl to rack and let cool. Dust top of cake with confectioners' sugar and serve warm or at room temperature with blueberries.

IN THE KITCHEN
When cooking in bowls or baking dishes in the slow cooker, make sure there's at least 1 inch between the side of the bowl and the stoneware. If it's too tight, there will be insufficient room for the heat to circulate, resulting in a flat or undercooked dessert.

PER SERVING (1 cup pudding with 2 tablespoons blueberries): 177 Cal, 5 g Fat, 2 g Sat Fat, 0 g Trans Fat, 113 mg Chol, 152 mg Sod, 29 g Carb, 1 g Fib, 5 g Prot, 68 mg Calc. *POINTS* value: *4.*

Apple-Rum Raisin Bread Pudding

prep 20 min • **slow-cook** 2 hrs • **serves** 8

4 cups cubed day-old crusty bread (1-inch pieces)

♦ 2 large apples, peeled and coarsely chopped (about 3 cups)

½ cup golden raisins

2 cups low-fat (1%) milk

1 cup fat-free half-and-half

½ cup packed brown sugar

♦ 2 large eggs

♦ 1 large egg white

1 tablespoon dark rum or ½ teaspoon rum extract

2 teaspoons vanilla extract

½ teaspoon cinnamon

½ teaspoon ground nutmeg

1 tablespoon confectioners' sugar

1 Spray 5- or 6-quart slow cooker stoneware with nonstick spray. Add bread cubes, apples, and raisins; toss to combine. Whisk milk, half-and-half, brown sugar, eggs, egg white, rum, vanilla, cinnamon, and nutmeg in large bowl; pour into slow cooker. Cover slow cooker tightly with foil, then place lid on top. Cook until toothpick inserted into center of pudding comes out clean, about 2 hours on high or 4 hours on low.

2 Transfer stoneware to rack and let pudding cool 15 minutes. Run thin knife around pudding to loosen it from stoneware. Invert onto large serving plate. Serve warm or at room temperature, dusted with confectioners' sugar.

IN THE KITCHEN

For the same *POINTS* value, this comfort classic is equally delicious prepared with an equal amount of pears and brandy in lieu of the apples and rum.

PER SERVING (³/₄ cup): 203 Cal, 3 g Fat, 1 g Sat Fat, 0 g Trans Fat, 55 mg Chol, 190 mg Sod, 41 g Carb, 2 g Fib, 5 g Prot, 83 mg Calc. *POINTS* value: **4.**

Rice Pudding with Indian Spices

2   cups low-fat (1%) milk

1   cup basmati or other long-grain rice

1/2 cup golden raisins

1/4 cup sugar

2   tablespoons light stick butter, melted

1/2 teaspoon vanilla extract

1/2 teaspoon ground cardamom

1   (4-inch) cinnamon stick

1 Spray 3 1/2- or 4-quart slow cooker stoneware with nonstick spray. Add milk, rice, raisins, sugar, melted butter, vanilla, and cardamom; mix well. Stir in cinnamon stick. Cover and cook until rice is very soft and mixture is thick and creamy, 2–2 1/2 hours on high or 4–5 hours on low.

2 Remove cinnamon stick. Serve warm or at room temperature.

♦ **FILLING EXTRA**
Serve each portion of this luscious pudding with 1/2 sliced large banana and up the **POINTS** value by **1.**

PER SERVING (3/4 cup): 229 Cal, 3 g Fat, 2 g Sat Fat, 0 g Trans Fat, 9 mg Chol, 61 mg Sod, 47 g Carb, 1 g Fib, 5 g Prot, 111 mg Calc.
POINTS value: **5.**

Peach-Blackberry Cobbler

prep 15 min • **microwave/slow-cook** 2 hrs 35 min • **serves** 6

♦ 2 (16-ounce) bags frozen sliced peaches, thawed

♦ 2 (6-ounce) containers fresh blackberries

3 tablespoons + 3 teaspoons sugar

Juice of 1/2 lemon

1 tablespoon cornstarch

3/4 cup all-purpose flour

1/2 teaspoon salt

1/2 teaspoon baking powder

1/4 teaspoon baking soda

1/3 cup low-fat buttermilk

2 tablespoons light stick butter, melted

1 teaspoon vanilla extract

1 Place small rack in bottom of 6-quart slow cooker.

2 To make filling, combine peaches, blackberries, 3 tablespoons sugar, lemon juice, and cornstarch in 1 1/2- to 2-quart round microwavable casserole. Cover with wax paper. Microwave on High until mixture is bubbling and starts to thicken, about 7 minutes, stirring once halfway through cooking time.

3 Meanwhile, to make topping, whisk flour, 2 1/2 teaspoons sugar, salt, baking powder, and baking soda in medium bowl. Stir in buttermilk and melted butter just until blended. Drop dough by tablespoonfuls onto hot filling, making 6 mounds. Sprinkle with remaining 1/2 teaspoon sugar.

4 Transfer casserole to rack in slow cooker. Cover and cook until toothpick inserted into center of each biscuit comes out clean, about 2 1/2 hours on high.

PER SERVING (1/3 cup filling with 1 biscuit): 180 Cal, 2 g Fat, 1 g Sat Fat, 0 g Trans Fat, 5 mg Chol, 312 mg Sod, 37 g Carb, 5 g Fib, 4 g Prot, 61 mg Calc. *POINTS* value: *3.*

Apricot-Almond Crisp

prep 15 min • slow-cook 4 hrs • serves 6

- ◆ 1/2 cup quick-cooking oats
- 1/3 cup packed brown sugar
- 1/4 cup all-purpose flour
- 1/4 cup toasted wheat germ
- 1/4 cup whole blanched almonds, finely chopped
- 1 tablespoon cold butter
- ◆ 1 to 2 tablespoons fat-free milk
- 1 tablespoon granulated sugar
- 3/4 teaspoon ground ginger
- 2 (14-ounce) cans apricot halves in juice, drained and cut in half
- 3/4 teaspoon almond extract

1 Spray 5- or 6-quart slow cooker stoneware with nonstick spray.

2 To make topping, combine oats, brown sugar, flour, wheat germ, and almonds in medium bowl. With fork, cut in butter until mixture resembles coarse crumbs. Gradually add milk, tossing lightly with fork, just until mixture resembles fine crumbs.

3 Mix granulated sugar and ginger in medium bowl. Add apricots and almond extract; toss to coat. Transfer apricot mixture to slow cooker. Sprinkle with topping; lightly spray with nonstick spray. Cover and cook until topping is crisp and begins to brown, about 4 hours on low.

IN THE KITCHEN
Top each serving with 1/4 cup fat-free vanilla frozen yogurt and 1 teaspoon chopped crystallized ginger and up the *POINTS* value by *1.*

PER SERVING (1/2 cup): 219 Cal, 6 g Fat, 2 g Sat Fat, 0 g Trans Fat, 5 mg Chol, 25 mg Sod, 39 g Carb, 4 g Fib, 5 g Prot, 46 mg Calc.
POINTS value: *4.*

"Baked" Apples with Gingersnaps

prep 15 min • **slow-cook** 3 hrs • **serves** 8

♦ 4   large Granny Smith or Rome Beauty apples

8   (2-inch) gingersnap cookies, coarsely crushed (about $1/2$ cup)

$1/4$ cup packed brown sugar

$1/4$ teaspoon cinnamon

Juice of 1 lemon

1   cup apple cider

1   tablespoon cold butter, cut into small pieces

2   tablespoons honey

1 Peel top half of each apple. With melon baller, cut out apple cores without cutting all the way through apples. Trim bottoms, if necessary, to stand apples upright.

2 Combine cookie crumbs, brown sugar, cinnamon, and half of lemon juice in small bowl. Fill apple cavities evenly with crumb mixture.

3 Transfer apples to 5- or 6-quart slow cooker. Pour cider and remaining lemon juice over apples. Dot apples evenly with butter and drizzle with honey. Cover slow cooker tightly with foil, then place lid on top. Cook until apples are fork-tender but still hold their shape, 3–3$1/2$ hours on low. Serve with cooking liquid.

IN THE KITCHEN

To crush the gingersnaps, place the cookies in a small zip-close plastic bag and gently pound them with a rolling pin or the bottom of a small skillet.

PER SERVING ($1/2$ stuffed apple with $1/2$ tablespoon cooking liquid): 155 Cal, 2 g Fat, 1 g Sat Fat, 0 g Trans Fat, 4 mg Chol, 58 mg Sod, 35 g Carb, 3 g Fib, 1 g Prot, 23 mg Calc. *POINTS* value: *3.*

Spiced Applesauce

- ◆ 6 Newton Pippin or other green apples, peeled and sliced
- 1/3 cup tiny red cinnamon candies
- 1/4 cup packed brown sugar
- Juice of 1/2 lemon
- 1/4 teaspoon cinnamon
- Pinch ground cloves
- Pinch salt
- 18 tiny red cinnamon candies, for garnish

1 Combine apples, 1/3 cup candies, brown sugar, lemon juice, cinnamon, cloves, and salt in 4-quart slow cooker. Press apples down so they form even layer. Cover and cook until mixture simmers and apples break apart, 4 hours on high or 8 hours on low.

2 At end of cooking time, let mixture cool 5 minutes. Coarsely mash apples with potato masher or puree in batches in blender or food processor. Garnish each serving with 3 candies. Serve warm or chilled.

◆ **FILLING EXTRA**
In addition to the candy garnish, top each serving of applesauce with 1 tablespoon fat-free sour cream then sprinkle with a pinch of freshly grated nutmeg.

PER SERVING (1/2 cup): 122 Cal, 0 g Fat, 0 g Sat Fat, 0 g Trans Fat, 0 mg Chol, 27 mg Sod, 32 g Carb, 3 g Fib, 0 g Prot, 14 mg Calc.
POINTS value: *2.*

Raspberry-Rhubarb Compote

prep 15 min • **cook/slow-cook** 2 hrs 30 min • **serves** 4

- 3 cups sliced fresh or thawed frozen rhubarb
- ³/₄ cup water
- ¹/₃ cup sugar
- ¹/₄ cup honey
- 1 tablespoon quick-cooking tapioca
- 2 (6-ounce) containers fresh raspberries

Grated zest of 1 lemon

- 1 tablespoon finely chopped crystallized ginger
- ¹/₂ teaspoon cinnamon
- ¹/₂ teaspoon vanilla extract

1 Combine rhubarb, water, sugar, honey, and tapioca in 4-quart slow cooker. Press mixture down so it forms even layer. Cover and cook until rhubarb is fork-tender, 2¹/₂ hours on high or 5 hours on low.

2 About 35 minutes before cooking time is up, stir in raspberries, lemon zest, ginger, and cinnamon. Cover and cook on high until mixture begins to simmer and raspberries are tender, about 30 minutes.

3 At end of cooking time, stir in vanilla until blended. Serve warm or at room temperature.

IN THE KITCHEN

Stuck with rock-hard crystallized ginger? Place it in a sieve set over a small saucepan of simmering water. Cover and steam until softened, about 5 minutes.

PER SERVING (about ³/₄ cup): 191 Cal, 0 g Fat, 0 g Sat Fat, 0 g Trans Fat, 0 mg Chol, 8 mg Sod, 49 g Carb, 6 g Fib, 2 g Prot, 206 mg Calc.
POINTS value: *3.*

Vanilla Custards with Lavender-Rosemary Drizzle

prep 15 min • microwave/cook/slow-cook 1 hr 5 min • serves 4

1   (3-inch) sprig fresh rosemary
    or 1 tablespoon dried

1   (3-inch) sprig fresh lavender
    or 1 tablespoon dried

4   tablespoons honey

1   vanilla bean

1   (12-ounce) can low-fat
    evaporated milk

1/2 cup low-fat (1%) milk

♦ 2   large eggs

♦ 2   large egg whites

1/4 cup sugar

1/8 teaspoon salt

1 Preheat heating base of 6-quart slow cooker to high.

2 Remove leaves from fresh rosemary and buds from fresh lavender. Combine rosemary leaves, lavender buds, and honey in small microwavable bowl. Microwave on High 30 seconds. Let stand until flavors are blended, about 5 minutes. Strain honey mixture through sieve into another small bowl and discard herbs.

3 With small, sharp knife, split vanilla bean lengthwise and scrape out seeds (reserve bean for another use such as making vanilla sugar). Combine evaporated milk, low-fat milk, 2 tablespoons honey mixture, and vanilla-bean seeds in small saucepan. Cook over medium heat until small bubbles appear around edge of pan, about 3 minutes. Let cool slightly, about 5 minutes.

4 Whisk eggs, egg whites, sugar, and salt in medium bowl. Slowly add hot milk mixture, whisking constantly, in thin steady stream. Pour mixture evenly into 4 (6-ounce) custard cups or ramekins. Place cups in stoneware and place it in heating base; add enough boiling water to stoneware to come halfway up outsides of cups. Cover and cook until each custard is set in center and jiggles slightly, 1–1 1/2 hours.

5 Carefully transfer custards to racks and let cool completely. Serve, drizzled with remaining 2 tablespoons honey mixture.

IN THE KITCHEN

These luscious custards can be made ahead. Cover and refrigerate up to 3 days.

PER SERVING (1 custard with 1/2 tablespoon honey): 266 Cal, 6 g Fat,
3 g Sat Fat, 0 g Trans Fat, 122 mg Chol, 239 mg Sod, 41 g Carb, 0 g Fib,
12 g Prot, 293 mg Calc. *POINTS* value: 6.

Spicy Chocolate-Orange Flan

prep 20 min • **cook/slow-cook** 1 hr 50 min • **serves** 8

1 cup sugar

Juice of 1/2 small lemon or 1 tablespoon water

1 (12-ounce) can low-fat evaporated milk

1/2 cup low-fat (1%) milk

1/2 cup semisweet chocolate chips, melted

1 (4-inch) cinnamon stick

1/8 teaspoon cayenne

♦ 2 large eggs

♦ 2 large egg whites

1/2 teaspoon vanilla extract

1/2 teaspoon orange extract

1/8 teaspoon salt

1 Preheat heating base of 5- or 6-quart slow cooker to high.

2 Combine 1/2 cup sugar and lemon juice in small heavy saucepan. Cook over medium heat, stirring constantly, until sugar is dissolved. Bring to boil. Cook, stirring occasionally, until it turns a deep golden caramel, about 10 minutes. Pour hot caramel into bottom of 2-quart soufflé dish. Quickly tilt dish so that bottom and halfway up side are coated with caramel.

3 Combine evaporated milk, low-fat milk, remaining 1/2 cup sugar, melted chocolate, cinnamon stick, and cayenne in medium saucepan. Cook over medium heat until small bubbles appear around edge of pan, about 5 minutes. Let cool slightly, about 5 minutes. Remove cinnamon stick.

4 Whisk eggs, egg whites, vanilla and orange extracts, and salt in medium bowl. Slowly add hot milk mixture, whisking constantly, in thin steady stream. Pour mixture into prepared dish and tightly cover with foil. Place dish in stoneware and place it in heating base; add enough boiling water to stoneware to come halfway up outside of dish. Cover and cook until center of flan is set and jiggles slightly, about 1 1/2 hours.

5 Carefully transfer dish to rack and let cool completely. Cover and refrigerate until completely chilled, at least 4 hours or overnight. Run thin knife around flan to loosen it from dish. Invert onto large serving plate, scraping out any extra caramel sauce from bottom of dish. Cut flan into 8 wedges and serve with caramel sauce.

PER SERVING (1 wedge with about 1 tablespoon sauce): 224 Cal, 6 g Fat, 3 g Sat Fat, 0 g Trans Fat, 61 mg Chol, 120 mg Sod, 37 g Carb, 1 g Fib, 7 g Prot, 147 mg Calc. **POINTS** value: **5.**

Summer Berry Parfaits

prep 10 min • **slow-cook** 1 hr • **serves** 8

♦ 1   (1 pound) container fresh strawberries, hulled and quartered

♦ 1   (6-ounce) container fresh blueberries

♦ 1   (6-ounce) container fresh blackberries

♦ 1   (6-ounce) container fresh raspberries

1/3   cup sugar

1/4   cup water

Juice of 1 small lemon

1   tablespoon cassis or other fruit brandy

1   (8-ounce) package fat-free cream cheese, at room temperature

1   cup plain low-fat (2%) Greek yogurt

1   teaspoon vanilla extract

1   (12-ounce) plain angel food cake, cut into 1/2-inch cubes

8   fresh mint leaves, thinly sliced

1 Combine berries, sugar, water, lemon juice, and cassis in 5- or 6-quart slow cooker. Cover and cook until berries are softened and mixture is juicy, 1–1 1/2 hours on low. Transfer berry mixture to large bowl and let cool.

2 Whisk cream cheese, yogurt, and vanilla in medium bowl until smooth. Alternately layer one eighth of cake cubes and berry mixture in each of 8 parfait glasses. Top evenly with yogurt mixture and mint.

IN THE KITCHEN

Greek yogurt is sought after for its rich, velvety texture, similar to that of sour cream or crème fraîche. It is thick and creamy because it has been strained of its whey during processing. The sheep's milk variety has a distinctive sour tang while the cow's milk version is milder. Both make equally delicious toppers on these refreshing fruit parfaits.

PER SERVING (1 parfait with scant 2 tablespoons yogurt mixture): 256 Cal, 1 g Fat, 1 g Sat Fat, 0 g Trans Fat, 4 mg Chol, 497 mg Sod, 52 g Carb, 4 g Fib, 10 g Prot, 134 mg Calc. *POINTS* value: *4.*

SOUTHWEST STEAK
TACOS, PAGE 39

Recipe Index

Recipes by *POINTS* value

0 *POINTS* value
Chayote with Five-Spice Sauce, 178

1 *POINTS* value
Beets with Dried Cherries, 180
Caponata, 25
Fennel and Onions with Saffron, 177
Green Beans Olivada, 181
Mini Falafels, 24

2 *POINTS* value
Baja Shrimp Boil, 22
Black Bean Salsa Dip, 26
Broccoli Frittata Bites, 23
Chicken, Apple, and Cheese Meatballs, 20
Hot Chocolate Latte, 31
Italian Snack Mix, 30
Lemon-Glazed Carrots and Parsnips, 179
Moo Shu Rolls, 18
Southern Artichoke Dip, 29
Spiced Applesauce, 191

3 *POINTS* value
African Peanut Chicken, 88
"Baked" Apples with Gingersnaps, 190
Cauliflower and Lentils with Feta, 169
Corn and Bacon Chowder, 123
Leeks with Dill Sauce, 175
Mixed-Grain Quick Bread, 158
Mumbai Chai, 32
Monkfish Ragù, 135
Peach-Blackberry Cobbler, 188

Pork-Pineapple Skewers, 19
Raspberry-Rhubarb Compote, 192
Spiced Apple-Nut Bread, 159
Squash and Cranberry Soup with Yogurt Drizzle, 174
Tomatillo-Pinto Bean Dip, 27
Warm Cheese and Cannellini Dip, 28
White Vegetable Soup, 173
Zesty Sausage and Tomato, 21

4 *POINTS* value
Apple-Rum Raisin Bread Pudding, 186
Apricot-Almond Crisp, 189
Brandy Chicken with Dried Plums and Olives, 131
Broccoflower and Cheese Soup, 168
Carrot Cake, 184
Classic Chicken Noodle Soup, 81
Cod Vera Cruz, 134
Corned Beef with Beet Relish, 112
Glogg, 33
Hearty Beef and Vegetable Soup, 46
Indian Lamb Curry, 124
Lamb with Stout, 125
Lemon Sponge Pudding with Blueberries, 185
Minestrone, 172
Osso Buco–Style Drumsticks, 95
Root Vegetable Tagine, 137
Rotisserie-Style Chicken, 76
"Sausage"-Stuffed Eggplant, 166
Summer Berry Parfaits, 195
Thai Chicken and Squash Soup, 129
Thai-Style Chicken Thighs, 89

Tofu Vegetable Stew, 164
Vegetable Sancocho, 176
White Balsamic Chicken, 128

5 *POINTS* value
Beef Burgoo, 48
Belgian Beef Stew, 44
Catalan Seafood Stew, 150
Bulgur and Bean Chili, 154
Cheese and Spinach–Stuffed Savoy Cabbage, 167
Chicken Mole, 130
Chicken, Sausage, and White Bean Stew, 92
Cider Pork Chops with Sage, 122
Country Captain Chicken, 77
Cranberry-Orange Turkey, 103
Creamy Turkey Meatballs, 104
Double Mushroom–Smothered Pork Chops, 59
Greens and Black-Eyed Peas, 170
Ham and Vegetable Chowder, 66
Harvest Pot Roast Dinner, 36
Hot-and-Spicy Turkey Curry, 100
Kentucky Pork Chili, 65
Kung Pao Chicken, 86
Lamb and Spinach Stew, 70
Latin-Style Meatball Soup, 51
Lentil-Winter Squash Stew, 157
Mexicali Turkey Breast, 98
Mexi-Style Meatball Soup, 133
Moussaka, 126
Mushroom and Cheese–Stuffed Chicken Breasts, 85

Dry and Liquid Measurement Equivalents

If you are converting the recipes in this book to metric measurements, use the following chart as a guide.

TEASPOONS	TABLESPOONS	CUPS	FLUID OUNCES
3 teaspoons	1 tablespoon		1/2 fluid ounce
6 teaspoons	2 tablespoons	1/8 cup	1 fluid ounce
8 teaspoons	2 tablespoons plus 2 teaspoons	1/6 cup	
12 teaspoons	4 tablespoons	1/4 cup	2 fluid ounces
15 teaspoons	5 tablespoons	1/3 cup minus 1 teaspoon	
16 teaspoons	5 tablespoons plus 1 teaspoon	1/3 cup	
18 teaspoons	6 tablespoons	1/4 cup plus 2 tablespoons	3 fluid ounces
24 teaspoons	8 tablespoons	1/2 cup	4 fluid ounces
30 teaspoons	10 tablespoons	1/2 cup plus 2 tablespoons	5 fluid ounces
32 teaspoons	10 tablespoons plus 2 teaspoons	2/3 cup	
36 teaspoons	12 tablespoons	3/4 cup	6 fluid ounces
42 teaspoons	14 tablespoons	1 cup minus 2 tablespoons	7 fluid ounces
45 teaspoons	15 tablespoons	1 cup minus 1 tablespoon	
48 teaspoons	16 tablespoons	1 cup	8 fluid ounces

TEASPOONS	
1/4 teaspoon	1 milliliter
1/2 teaspoon	2 milliliters
1 teaspoon	5 milliliters
1 tablespoon	15 milliliters
2 tablespoons	30 milliliters
3 tablespoons	45 milliliters
1/4 cup	60 milliliters
1/3 cup	80 milliliters
1/2 cup	120 milliliters
2/3 cup	160 milliliters
3/4 cup	175 milliliters
1 cup	240 milliliters
1 quart	950 milliliters

LENGTH	
1 inch	25 millimeters
1 inch	2.5 centimeters

WEIGHT	
1 ounce	30 grams
1/4 pound	120 grams
1/2 pound	240 grams
1 pound	480 grams

OVEN TEMPERATURE			
250°F	120°C	400°F	200°C
275°F	140°C	425°F	220°C
300°F	150°C	450°F	230°C
325°F	160°C	475°F	250°C
350°F	180°C	500°F	260°C
375°F	190°C	525°F	270°C

Note: Measurement of less than 1/8 teaspoon is considered a dash or a pinch. Metric volume measurements are approximate.